TYPE CAST

Creative Page Design
Using Words, Type and Letters

FROM THE EDITORS OF
MEMORY MAKERS BOOKS

11 10 09 08 07   5 4 3 2 1

Distributed in Canada by Fraser Direct
100 Armstrong Avenue
Georgetown, ON, Canada L7G 5S4
Tel: (905) 877-4411

Distributed in the U.K. and Europe by David & Charles
Brunel House, Newton Abbot, Devon, TQ12 4PU, England
Tel: (+44) 1626 323200, Fax: (+44) 1626 323319
E-mail: postmaster@davidandcharles.co.uk

Distributed in Australia by Capricorn Link
P.O. Box 704, S. Windsor, NSW 2756 Australia
Tel: (02) 4577-3555

Library of Congress Cataloging-in-Publication Data

Type cast : creative page design using words, type and letters / from the editors of Memory Makers Books.
      p. cm.
  Includes index.
  ISBN-13: 978-1-59963-003-8 (pbk.: alk.paper)
  ISBN-10: 1-59963-003-6 (pbk.: alk.paper)
  1. Photograph albums. 2. Scrapbooks. 3. Type and type-founding. I. Memory Makers Books.
TR501.T97 2007
745.593--dc22
                          2006036816

Editor: Karen Davis
Writer: Darlene D'Agostino
Designer: Marissa Bowers
Layout Artist: Anne Shannon
Art Coordinator: Eileen Aber
Production Coordinator: Matt Wagner
Photographer: Al Parrish
Stylist: Jan Nickum

CONTRIBUTING ARTISTS

Amber Baley — *Memory Makers Master 2006*

Joanna Bolick — *Memory Makers Master 2004*

Vicki Boutin

Karen Davis

Kathy Fesmire — *Memory Makers Master 2004*

Becky Fleck

Greta Hammond

Linda Harrison

Barb Hogan

Kim Kesti

Sharon Laakkonen

Heather Preckel

Jessica Sprague — *Memory Makers Master 2006*

Shannon Taylor — *Memory Makers Master 2005*

KLMNOPQRSTUVWXYZ

BELLE

Summer 2004

is such a Good dog.

From day 1 she's been

a protector And Friend.

Introduction

In the book *Understanding Media*, author Marshall McLuhan wrote, "the medium is the message." While he was concerned with broader and more complicated ideas about how society interprets and reacts to information, we, as scrapbook-page designers, should adopt this statement.

With a scrapbook page, you have the opportunity to make someone stop and think. You have the power to provoke thought through words of wisdom, words of art. The type on your page adds meaning and emotion, and hand-in-hand with the photos, it defines the layout. Type occupies the best supporting role on your layout. It deserves its own creative process.

Think about your scrapbooking supplies for a minute. How many lettering products do you have on hand, at your fingertips, ready to be used to full capacity? Letter stickers, lettering templates, letter stamps, letter rub-ons, letter punches, letter-patterned paper, word and phrase stickers, preprinted transparencies! Oh, and my word, how many *fonts* do you own? These are powerful tools, and with this book comes the empowering confidence to use them with effect.

Mission No. 1 is the message: how to use words to your advantage. Capture your thoughts and corral them into titles and text. Mission No. 2 is the medium: how to portray these words with unbridled creativity. These words should partner with everything on your page—photos, colors, mood, theme. Type is the ultimate unifying element, and as you consider how to use it on your page, remember that the medium is just as important as the message.

i ♥ heart you

alek + grace

To have a loving relationship with a sister is not simply to have a buddy or a confidant — it is to have a soulmate for life.
—Victoria Secunda

CHAPTER 1

Ta-Ta to Typical Titles

After the photos, the title plays second fiddle to none in regard to page presence. A title has real job security. A title grabs the eye by the shirt collar. Through color, contrast and pattern effects, it says, "Dear reader, you should really be feeling like *this* when you look at this scrapbook page." But its highest calling is connectivity, since the title is the page element that connects the photos to the story and the reader to the page. If a scrapbook page were a party, the title would play a perfectionist hostess, setting the mood and introducing the reader to the story through meaning, and by giving her eye a solid starting point.

Titles offer not-to-be-missed opportunities for creativity. The smallest tweaks in placement can give a scrapbook page an entirely different energy, leaving you, the artist, asking yourself, "Whoa! What just happened?" Whatever it was, though, you liked it! Letters can be accessorized with theme-enforcing accents. Baselines (Not sure what those are? Well, not to worry. You'll learn soon enough.) can be aligned to fit any number of moods. Artistic media (you know, the stuff you use, like stamps and chalk, to make pretty things) can be mixed to create an exciting visual landscape. Letter size can be adjusted to over-, under- and properly state any emotion.

Now that we've blah-blah-blahed enough about how great titles are, we'll show you how to make your own titles great. Commence page turning!

Smoosh

Sharon Laakkonen, Superior, Wisconsin

This title bounces along its baseline. Baseline--remember we mentioned that in this chapter's introduction and said we'd explain? The baseline is the imaginary line on which text runs. Text can run along it in nice, neat, deliberate steps or it can practically ignore its existence by bouncing up above and drooping far below it. Here, a few letter stickers highlighted by size dip a little below the baseline. The dipping works in conjunction with the tight letter spacing to make the letters look squeezed and squished together, conveying the "smooshed" theme.

Supplies: Patterned paper (Polar Bear Press); flowers (Prima); brads, acrylic flowers (Queen & Co.); letter stickers (Imagination Project); thread; pen; cardstock

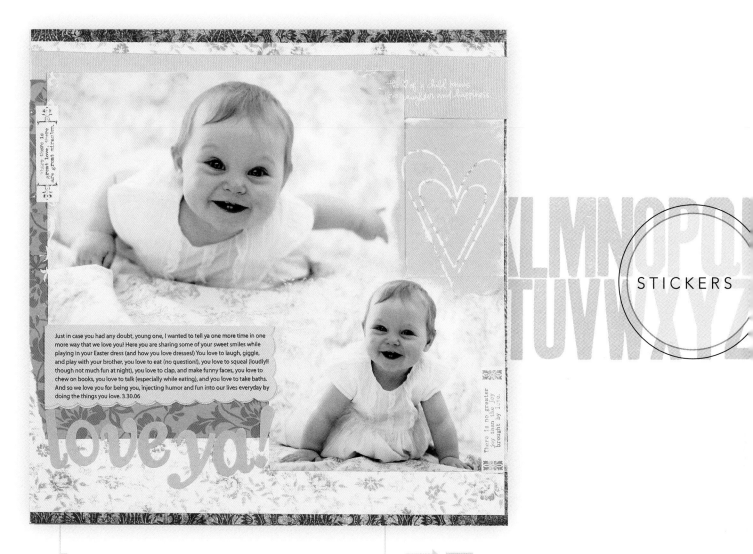

Everything about this layout is soft and feminine. It perfectly expresses the gentle smile of a baby girl dressed in her pretty Easter dress and posed on top of toile fabric. The lowercase letter stickers impart an informal mood while the gracious curves of the letter style flirt with the reader. The letters bridge the meeting of two pieces of patterned paper with a connecting layer of pink. The simple title was created to complement in an understated and somewhat refined way.

Supplies: Patterned paper (Anna Griffin, BasicGrey, Melissa Frances); ribbon (Strano); heart mask (Heidi Swapp); acrylic paint; letter stickers (Making Memories); narrative stickers (Creative Imaginations); rub-ons (Melissa Frances); cardstock

I Love Ya!

Joanna Bolick, Fletcher, North Carolina

Power Up

Kim Kesti, Phoenix, Arizona

What's Your Type?

Looking for fresh ideas for integrating type into your scrapbook? Just look around you. Typefaces are everywhere. Try "borrowing" font and design ideas from unconventional sources and adapting them to your own scrapbooking style. Here are five places to look:

- **Graphic T-shirts**
- **Product Packaging**
- **Your DVD Collection**
- **Corporate Logos**
- **Display Advertising**

ABCDEFGHIJKLMNOPQRSTUVWXYZ

Movement is the name of this game. Bold, black letter stickers with a simple mix of lettering styles and sizes add to the kinetic energy that moves across this page. The title words create a visual triangle that frames a vibrant sunflower that contrasts beautifully against a strong blue sky. The idea of "power" is the heart and soul of this layout. The photos show power in its many forms, from the presence of actual power lines to the more subtle concepts of powering a car with gas or a body with food and caffeine.

Supplies: Patterned paper (Urban Lily); chipboard shapes (Deluxe Designs); acrylic paint; letter stickers (source unknown); pen; marker; cardstock

the oaks family are always FEARLESS when it comes to their annual Jeep adventure in MOAB Utah. No rock is too big, no slope is too steep.

Excuse us, but how effective are the brakes on this thing? The striking imagery of the SUV seemingly defying the laws of gravity calls for a striking title. A mix of colorful and stylistically unique letter stickers delivers. (By the way, this technique is an excellent way to use leftover letter stickers.) The colorful arrangement helps to connect the photo with the eclectic pattern of the background paper. Aptly placed in the upper right of the photo, the title adds balance by filling in an empty space within the photo.

Supplies: Patterned paper (Imagination Project); stickers (American Crafts, Arctic Frog, Creative Imaginations, EK Success, Imagination Project, Scenic Route Paper Co.); pen; image editing software (Adobe)

No Fear

Barb Hogan, Cincinnati, Ohio

Rush

Becky Fleck
Columbus, Montana

Never underestimate the power of a subtitle. On this page, a single word written in simply styled letter stickers creates an elegant title. The large type and contrast of white against lavender instantly grabs the eye and pulls it into the journaling. As the eye travels across the page, it is halted by a spinning page element that expresses the lovely thrill of a swing by simply saying "wheeeeeeeee!" The curving connectedness of the "whee" letters express the motion and joy of the ride. The central and circular design of the element connects the pattern-blocked background, thereby unifying the page.

Supplies: Patterned paper (Heidi Grace Designs); chipboard (Fancy Pants Designs); acrylic paint; letter stickers (American Crafts); circle cutter; cardstock; Willing Race font (Harold's Fonts)

To earn the WHITE HELMET, you need to be the class sparring

the **WHITE** ★ helmet

Champion and Shannon did it! She might not hold the honor very long, but it's good while it lasts!

STICKERS

Can we get a "HI-YAH!" for excellently employed color contrast and symbolism within a title? The colors in the photo are varied and bright. A neutral background energized with blocks and strips of patterned paper is an appropriate choice that also produces a challenge: how to create a commanding title that does not overpower and does not get lost in the energy. Enter a short and simple letter-sticker title with high color contrast and a highlighted word. The funky baseline alignment of each word adds to the energy of the page.

Supplies: Patterned paper (KI Memories); letter stickers (American Crafts, Arctic Frog); pen; marker; cardstock

White Helmet

Barb Hogan, Cincinnati, Ohio

Sunshine

Kim Kesti, Phoenix, Arizona

These letters have all the childlike vibrancy of a sidewalk-chalked hopscotch board. Originally just plain white, the stickers were inked with chalk stamping ink, allowed to dry and then adhered to the radiating rays of a paper sunshine. The paper sun is a direct link to the mini masterpiece shown in the photo. The less saturated primary and secondary colors of the letters, as well as the innocent mix of upper- and lowercase letters, instantly remind one of preschool fun and learning.

Supplies: Cardstock; letter stickers (American Crafts); chalk ink; buttons (Junkitz); pen

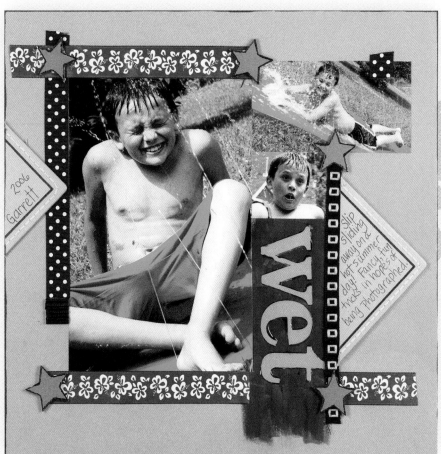

Wet

Shannon Taylor, Bristol, Tennessee

This title placement is anything but washed up. It exists within a bounty of layers and helps define the edges of the photos, thereby drawing attention to them. The high-contrast relationship between orange and blue along with the exaggerated size of the letters make the title cry out to the reader. The title is a resist image; it was created by brushing a wash of blue paint over removable letter stickers that were first applied to orange cardstock. Once dry, the stickers were removed and a layer of clear gloss medium was brushed on in their absence for a glistening effect.

Supplies: Cardstock; ribbons (KI Memories, Offray); chipboard stars (Li'l Davis Designs); chipboard coaster (source unknown); beads (Blumenthal); dimensional adhesive; ceramic paint; pen

Fun Font Facts

- Phototypesetting, the technology that transformed typesetting from the use of metal plates onto film negatives—thus significantly broadening typeface options—has been around only since the type revolution of the 1960s and '70s.

- Your Web browser, such as Netscape or Internet Explorer, limits its displays to the fonts that are installed on your computer—unless the Web designer took the time to convert the font on that particular page into an actual graphic through a process called embedding.

- Type designers have been known to use just about anything to create typefaces—from calligraphy pens to lipstick to spray paint.

Taking a Dip

Linda Harrison, Sarasota, Florida

Whoopsadaisy! Did your eye just slip down this title? This snaking effect tickles the eye with visual butterflies. Taking a literal dip of its own, the title follows the wavy design element with big, clear letters that provide top and bottom anchors for the page. The white, blocked, serifed letter stickers contrast against the green background while helping to brighten the white background of the patterned paper.

Supplies: Patterned paper, letter stickers (American Crafts); die-cut circles; pen; cardstock

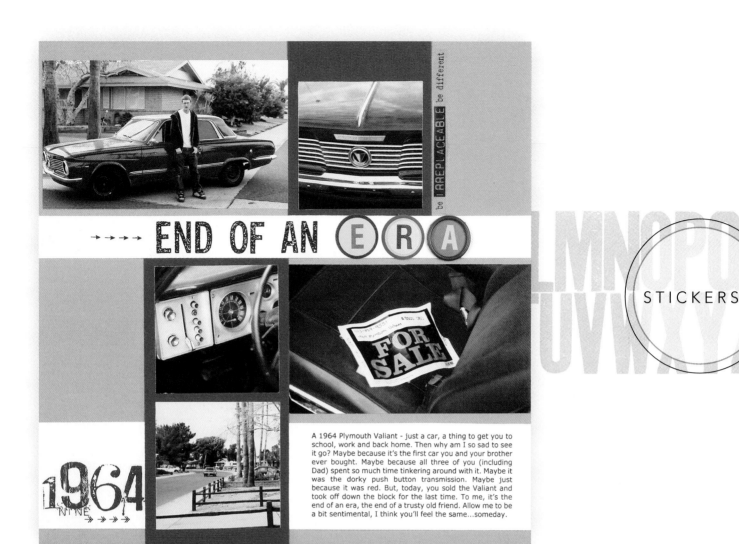

A 1964 Plymouth Valiant - just a car, a thing to get you to school, work and back home. Then why am I so sad to see it go? Maybe because it's the first car you and your brother ever bought. Maybe because all three of you (including Dad) spent so much time tinkering around with it. Maybe it was the dorky push button transmission. Maybe just because it was red. But, today, you sold the Valiant and took off down the block for the last time. To me, it's the end of an era, the end of a trusty old friend. Allow me to be a bit sentimental, I think you'll feel the same...someday.

That red. Cherry. Undeniable. Intoxicating. Dangerous. It can't be ignored, but paying too much attention to it could be a page design tragedy. So, subtlety becomes the strong suit of this title, using only enough red to support the photos. The circular letter stickers practically roll along the page, subliminally prodding the mind with images of tires and steering wheels. A single concho around the letter "a" adds a hint of dimension while the overall curvature helps soften the straight lines and right angles of the photos and journaling block. Paired with the grungy number stickers, you might feel a little road rash.

Supplies: Cardstock; letter stickers (American Crafts); rub-on letters (Making Memories); number stickers (Creative Imaginations); conchos (Scrapworks); Arial font (Microsoft)

End of an Era

Kim Kesti, Phoenix, Arizona

Kite Flying

Kathy Fesmire, Athens, Tennessee

This page carries all the excitement of a Chinese New Year celebration. Foam-stamped letters styled with thick, almost brushlike strokes match the look of the stamped Kangxi, or Chinese characters, background. Once stamped, the individual letters were cut into shapes that mimic a traditional kite. The edges were then inked with blue and red. Complementing and contrasting mats along with alternately adhering the letters with foam adhesive helps them pop off an exuberant background. The second half of the title was stamped as well; the letter styling is a ransom's mix of traditional typefaces. Together, they further the page's carnivalesque feel.

Supplies: Patterned paper (BasicGrey, Karen Foster Design, My Mind's Eye); journaling sleeve, letter stamps (EK Success); stamp, stamping ink, acrylic paint (Plaid); chipboard accent (BasicGrey); rub-ons (Making Memories); charms; ribbons (source unknown)

Tattoo

Kim Kesti, Phoenix, Arizona

Heeeey, hep cat. This layout is cool. No, it's so cool, it's hip. Wait, upon further reflection, you could call it grungy with its perfect imperfection (baseline alignment and letter spacing are just a bit off), distressing and raw emotion. However you label it, it's a perfect fit for a page about a toddler's first tattoo (yes, it's temporary!). The gritty, grainy letter stamp set is *the* vehicle to convey modern angst. The letters were individually cut and adhered with foam adhesive. Hipster-inspired line-rendered flourishes help accent and lend street cred (credibility, that is).

Supplies: Patterned paper (KI Memories, Provo Craft); rubber stamps (FontWerks); stamping ink; embossing powder; adhesive foam; pen; cardstock

Supplies: Patterned paper (Scenic Route Paper Co.); ledger paper (Making Memories); letter stamps (Heidi Swapp, Technique Tuesday); fabric flowers (Chatterbox, Doodlebug Designs); word tags (Making Memories); rhinestones (Westrim); large paper clip (Bazzill); rub-ons (My Mind's Eye); cardstock; Dinner and a Movie font (Scrap Supply)

Create Passion

Linda Harrison, Sarasota, Florida

This title is so large, so present, you feel obligated to obey it. Conventional scrapbooking wisdom will tell you photos should, nay, *must* be the focal point of the page. Here the idea laid forth in the title is the nucleus. The title is *the* largest thing on the page and therefore takes on a life of its own. Its avocado green background makes a definite statement while the stamped letters rest seamlessly over the playful polka-dot pattern. The architectural styling of the letters gives the word "create" a velocity.

APR 2006

WHEN CAM CHATS ONLINE WITH HIS FRIENDS, THIS IS THE IMAGE HE DISPLAYS. HE LIKES THAT HIS AVATAR LOOKS LIKE A SKATER—A TOUGH KID WITH A GLARING LOOK.

THE FIRST IMPRESSION THAT HE GIVES OTHERS, ALTHOUGH COOL — IN A 'GANGSTA' SORT OF WAY, IS NOT A TRUE REPRESENTATION OF CAM.

I'D LIKE OTHERS TO SEE THE KIND, SOFT-HEARTED BOY THAT I KNOW CAM TO BE. I'D LIKE HIS PICTURE TO HAVE A FRIENDLY SMILE AND AN INVITING LOOK. I'D LIKE HIS WARM, CARING PERSONALITY TO SHINE THROUGH THE SCREEN.

BUT, I'M JUST HIS MOM. WHAT DO I KNOW?

Not a True Story

Amber Baley, Waupun, Wisconsin

Supplies: Patterned paper (BasicGrey); rub-ons (7 Gypsies, Autumn Leaves); brads; metal tag (7 Gypsies); stamping ink; cardstock; Hootie font (Dafont)

At first glance, this title could be foreshadowing a juicy "E! Hollywood True Story" dish of dirt. Or, maybe we are to think that criminal details only found in a police investigation are sure to follow. This short title has a seamless layered effect, thanks to rub-ons. The word-on-word creates a visual statement by pairing a large, outline, block font with a gritty, sans-serif font of smaller stature. By itself, the squat-width title would be lacking, but a row of stars more than compensates for its length.

What do you get when you take a well-known phrase, spell it with bold lettering and wrap it with a tangy color combo? A title that jumps off an exciting background. The exciting background came to be after a quarter sheet of rub-ons was applied to a thick block of white cardstock. The title needed to be housed in an attention-getting element if it was to be noticeable. Drawing more attention to it is a strong, curving, red arrow.

Supplies: Patterned paper, rub-ons (Scenic Route Paper Co.); brads (Queen & Co.); circle cutter; adhesive foam; pen; cardstock

Play Hard

Vicki Boutin, Burlington, Ontario, Canada

Persuading Spring

Becky Fleck
Columbus, Montana

This title is as subtle as the daily changes in a blooming bulb. The page theme called for elements that were delicate and unobtrusive. These rub-ons have such a fine appearance; be careful or you might break them! The title, like the page, is softly asking spring to come, using friendly and pretty persuasion. Take a close look at the page background to see the exquisitely stitched flower accents.

Supplies: Patterned paper (Chatterbox); flowers, rub-on letters (Making Memories); chalk; beads; crystal lacquer

RUB-ONS

ABCDEFGHI
JKLMNOPQR

Photo Booth

Barb Hogan, Cincinnati, Ohio

Energy and excitement radiate from this title like a sun exploding with good times. Rub-ons, like stickers, allow total control in placement. For this title, that means letters are able to bounce up curves and overlap each other all in the name of fun. Polka dots are heavily employed on this page. The strong straight lines of the sun accent provide a wonderful contrast to the energy of the circles.

Supplies: Patterned paper (Doodlebug Design, KI Memories); chipboard shapes (Imagination Project); glitter dimensional paint (Ranger); rub-on letters (Scrapworks); pigment ink; pen; marker; cardstock

The Lazy Hazy
Days of Summer

Greta Hammond, Goshen, Indiana

Stickers or rub-ons? Oh, the choices a scrapbooker must make. Both come in a gazillion styles, sizes and colors. Both have their advantages, but with rub-ons, you never have to worry about them getting removed. This whimsical rub-on title flits across the page with the carefree attitude of summer, which is further emphasized with curving doodles. The large, chipboard flower accent separates the two adjectives in the title from the noun and brings the eye directly to the photo.

Supplies: Patterned paper (Fancy Pants Designs, SEI); chipboard flower (Fancy Pants Designs); chipboard bookplate, fabric flower (SEI); rub-ons (Doodlebug Designs, Provo Craft); acrylic paint; brads; buttons (Autumn Leaves); fabric tab (source unknown); rickrack; cardstock

Shake It Up!

When it comes to titles, traveling along the straight and narrow is for sissies! Okay, maybe that's a bit harsh. But, if you do little to add oomph to your title or historically place titles in the upper-left corner of your scrapbook page, get out of that comfort zone! These ideas will add energy to your pages!

- **Mix Letter Cases:** Throw traditional grammar rules out the window. Surprise the reader by placing a capital letter in the middle of a word. Or, try including a backward letter for zaniness.

- **Incorporate Images:** Try switching out a letter or even an entire word with a symbolic image. The letter "O" is a wonderful candidate for such substitution.

- **Mix the Media:** Combine metal letters with a flirty script font. Add a few stamped letters to a group of letter stickers. Use rub-ons with epoxy stickers. The possibilities are only limited by your imagination.

- **Highlight a Letter:** Color, size, shadows and type style are your friends for this technique. Pick a significant letter, whether that determination is based on mood or simply a matter of solid design, and give it permission to stand out.

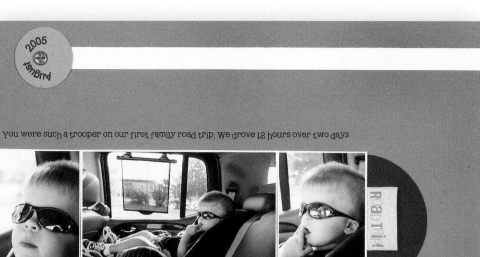

You were such a trooper on our first family road trip. We drove 12 hours over two days

to visit Grandpa in North Carolina. It was a great memory and we can't wait to do it again!

COMPUTER

On the Road

Linda Harrison, Sarasota, Florida

This title is the final stop in a repeating series of shapes. Circle shapes, more specifically, repeating circle shapes, create a definite sense of movement within a design. This is especially appropriate for a page about a mini road warrior. A screwtop brad anchors the title and propels the radiating movement of the title words. A simple but bold font keeps the title clean and noticeable.

Supplies: Cardstock; circle punch; die-cut shapes (QuicKutz); fabric tab (Scrapworks); brads (Karen Foster Design)

This enlarged detail shot perfectly captures the innocence, wonder and hope of a child at Christmas. "Jinging bells." It's the toddler boy's vocabulary for "jingle bells." Appropriating the phrase creates a sweet title that will hold a fleeting moment forever. Created with the help of image editing software, the repeating title text appears to vibrate from the swinging bell in the photo. Layering the text in varying opacities allows the reader to almost hear the reverberating decrescendo created from a jingling bell.

Supplies: Patterned paper (BasicGrey, Scenic Route Paper Co.); rub-on stitches (Die Cuts With A View); metal tag (Making Memories); ribbon (Maya Road); Snell Roundhand, Optima fonts (Internet download)

Jinging Bells

Joanna Bolick, Fletcher, North Carolina

The Hippo Slide was one of our favorite new attractions at Lakewood. We even talked Austin into taking a turn coming down the beachfront slide. He had just as much fun as the kids did as you can tell by the huge smile on his face. I am sure if the kids have anything to do with it, next year he will make more than one trip down the wet and wild water slide!

Hippo Slide

Kathy Fesmire, Athens, Tennessee

Wow! This handwriting is perfectly rendered! Well, it's not exactly handwriting; it's a collection of computer fonts with penmanship quality. The outline style of the large font begs to be filled in with watery blue brushstrokes. The childlike imperfection of the smaller font is perfectly imperfect.

Supplies: Patterned paper (My Mind's Eye); rub-on letters (Doodlebug Designs); ribbon (Offray); stamping ink; acrylic paint; staples; buttons (source unknown); paper glaze; pen; cardstock

I am so incredibly lucky! Two stores, The Scrapbook Shoppe in Tampa & Made for Memories in Sarasota, flew me to Florida to teach four classes. I felt like the luckiest girl in the world. They treated me like I was some kind of celebrity. They were so kind. I even stayed in a beautiful condo on the shores of the Gulf of Mexico. During my down time, I walked up & down the beach looking for seashells for my little guys. Then I fell in love with the colorful lifeguard stations. The primary colors just popped off the white sand. I knew I must photograph them. I still can't believe how lucky I am. April - 2006

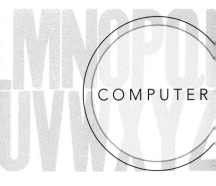

The rippling edges of these letters are characteristic of the font in which they were printed; the photographic backgrounds are not. With the help of image editing software, you can use photos to fill in the letters of a font, much like you'd add color to a block font. The title employs a panoramic photo showing the expanse of a shoreline. The edges of the 100% digital page mimic the edges of the font.

Supplies: Image editing software (Adobe); Bluecake, Mistress Script fonts (Internet download)

Lifeguard
Stations

Shannon Taylor, Bristol, Tennessee

Best Friends

Sharon Laakkonen, Superior, Wisconsin

Little pops of bright orange and green punctuate this title like wild flowers sprouting in a bed of grass. The foundation of the title is an elegant font printed directly on the photo. The computer-generated letters were used as a stitching guide. The thread follows curves similar to the organic shapes seen in the flourishes that edge the photo. The stitched vines signify the close-knit relationship between the two girls.

Supplies: Patterned paper (A2Z Essentials); digital brushes (Shabby Princess); velvet flowers (Prima); circle punch; distress ink; embroidery floss; beads (Michaels); cardstock

Ready, Set, Jump!

Greta Hammond, Goshen, Indiana

Employing size and color in the name of emphasis is easy with a computer, especially when you're creating a handcut title. A touch of a button here, a mouse click there and, poof! Just like magic. Here, the title was printed in reverse on the back of cardstock and then cut out. The gradient size of the letters that spell "jump" complements the rising action in the photo series. The title helps convey the idea of building excitement. When photographing an event, consider a photo series, which is an excellent way to show movement, action or a story arc.

Supplies: Patterned paper, coaster, tab (Imagination Project); die-cut letters (QuicKutz); button (Autumn Leaves); cardstock; Another Typewriter font (Dafont)

Banner Headlines!

Headline writers get paid big bucks for crafting attention-getting titles. Use their tricks of the trade to compose your own.

- **Free Associate:** With photos in hand, create a list of words that come to mind when you relive the memory. Think about the mood you wish to convey.

- **Common Sense:** Which of the five senses was most aroused by the memories? Did the home-cooked vittles overwhelm your sense of smell?

- **Oh, That's Punny!:** Puns will either make or break a title. Avoid tasteless puns and bad clichés. Instead, put a fresh spin on a weathered phrase.

- **Explain it to a Friend:** If you were going to explain the story behind your layout to a friend, what detail would you lead with? Fashion that into your page title.

Hidden within our everyday life

Are tiny spots of

light -

The moments of joy

I never knew were possible.

You teach me how to

find

them.

I love you.

Hidden Joy

Jessica Sprague, Cary, North Carolina

Through color and dimension, this title is bold and understated at the same time. The first half of the title is a little hidden in the design. It discreetly runs along the left side of the photo; its white letters seamlessly meld with the white photo background. Then, as the title turns the corner, it springs into action in the form of vibrant and supersaturated chipboard letters. The letters, contained in a matching pink set of brackets, dodge and weave with the edges of a supersized paper flourish. This handcut accent is an unconventional and exciting cropping mechanism.

Supplies: Patterned paper (K & Company, KI Memories); chipboard letters, rub-on letters (Heidi Swapp); rub-on accents (BasicGrey); flowers (Prima); acrylic bubbles (KI Memories); rhinestones; metal charm (Li'l Davis Designs)

We are never short of smiles and laughter whenever Grandma is around.

Her positive outlook and warm personality is contagious to everyone around her.

She loves to laugh and giggle with the two of you.

She finds a lot of joy just being with us and we love having her around.

Smile, Laugh, Giggle

Greta Hammond, Goshen, Indiana

These chipboard title letters make a statement with size and color. The smaller words, set in lowercase letters, allow the title to breathe and help balance the intensity of the larger, all uppercase word. Although the colors are fairly soft, being set against a dark chocolate background turns up the vibrancy volume. The colors also call out the interesting color combinations found in the patterned papers.

Supplies: Patterned paper (Imagination Project); chipboard letters (Heidi Swapp, Pressed Petals); acrylic paint; rubber stamps (Hero Arts); buttons (Autumn Leaves); rickrack; cardstock; Modern Type font (Autumn Leaves)

In Motion

**Heather Preckel,
Swannanoa, North Carolina**

Arrows, circle shapes and curving baselines come together to create a title that appears to be somersaulting across the page. The title is a perfect complement to a photo series that shows a brave boy executing daredevil flips while jumping on a trampoline. The lime, turquoise and orange color combination adds to the energy.

Supplies: Patterned paper (A2Z Essentials); chipboard letters (Heidi Swapp); pigment ink; circle cutter; pen; cardstock

You Crack Me Up

Shannon Taylor, Bristol, Tennessee

Chipboard, it's the strong, silent type. Its sturdiness lets it reach and stretch beyond page borders without an overwhelming fear that it might get bent. And at this size, it practically dares you to get creative. Embellish to your heart's content! It is the perfect canvas for heavier accents. Here, the letters are loaded with buttons. But before that, they were covered with cardstock and chalked.

Supplies: Patterned paper, chipboard accents (Junkitz); large chipboard letters (source unknown); small chipboard letters (Scenic Route Paper Co.); buttons (Autumn Leaves, Junkitz); acrylic paint; thread; pen

Grow

Becky Fleck, Columbus, Montana

There is something childlike and innocent about these large lowercase chipboard letters. The curves of the individual letters and exaggerated extenders offer a casual and natural feel, making the lettering style a perfect match for this dirt-digging page. The title gets added oomph when the letter "o" in "grow" is replaced with a handmade paper flower. More handmade paper flowers, doodles and polka dots keep the mood light.

Supplies: Patterned paper (Crate Paper); chipboard letters (Pressed Petals); brads (Making Memories); acrylic paint; thread; pen; cardstock

Cat + Leaf = Happy

Jessica Sprague, Cary, North Carolina

This page title is just one element in a collection that frames the photo. But, it is the element with the most contrast—a natural attention getter. These chipboard letters are outline only, meaning their blank centers are perfect for spicing up with patterned paper. The raw, natural look of the chipboard lends a casual, everyday feel to the page and just a tad of dimension.

Supplies: Patterned paper (K & Company, KI Memories, My Mind's Eye); chipboard accents (BasicGrey, Maya Road); foam stamps (Li'l Davis Designs); ribbon (American Crafts, Making Memories, SEI); digital brush (Designer Digitals); cardstock; CBX Farrell font (Chatterbox); Century Gothic, Impact fonts (Microsoft)

Happy Day

Heather Preckel, Swannanoa, North Carolina

Sandwiched between two thick lengths of patterned paper, this chipboard title skates across this card. It's large enough to hold its own among a mix of vibrant elements. The fact that half of the title is housed inside a handmade paper flower is an effective attention getter. Its white background color helps it pop against the background while the black outline provides needed definition.

Supplies: Patterned paper (A2Z Essentials); chipboard letters (Heidi Swapp); flower (Bazzill); circle punch; adhesive foam; pen

Hallmark was definitely onto something when it started the greeting card business. Cards are a quick and thoughtful way to let someone know you care, and that's especially true if the card is handmade. The large chipboard letter "h" on this card acts as a drop cap. It commands even more attention because it is covered in a paisley letter sticker. Solid letter stickers spell the remainder of the title and a line of brads provide punctuation.

Hello Card

Karen Davis, Hillsboro, Ohio

Supplies: Patterned paper (Fancy Pants Designs); chipboard letter (All My Memories); letter stickers (All My Memories, SEI); ribbons (Making Memories, May Arts); leather flower (Making Memories); brads; eyelet; pigment ink; cardstock

Crush

Kathy Fesmire, Athens, Tennessee

Like a banner headline in a newspaper or display advertising, this purple chipboard title grabs our attention by occupying the bottom third of this scrapbook page. The handcut letters were crafted in the same style as the soda logo, then painted the requisite purple and covered in a coat of clear gloss medium. The word, "Crush," also is repeated throughout the layout via accents and photos. This repetition creates a definite rhythm but also forms a visual triangle that helps guide the eye.

Supplies: Patterned paper (Bo-Bunny Press, Making Memories); rub-ons (Doodlebug Designs); brads, photo turns (Queen & Co.); flowers (Teters); ribbons; crystal lacquer; dye ink; buttons; "Crush" bottlecaps; cardstock

39

A Beautiful
Bridesmaid

Sharon Laakkonen, Superior, Wisconsin

Supplies: Patterned paper, rub-on letters (Imagination Project); acrylic letters (Heidi Swapp); flowers (Prima); beads (Michaels); clear adhesive; thread; pen; cardstock

Key letters are larger in this title that wraps around the photos. These larger letters move the eye along the splintered word and draw attention to points in the photos, such as the eyes. The letters also help contain the energy created by the layered, angled photos as well as the layered flower embellishment. Clear beads on top of the acrylic letters add elegance but with a sense of youthfulness. The letters were outlined with a white pen for definition.

All That Jazz

Titles are a natural candidate for glitz, dimension and decoration. Zing up a title with one of these ideas.

- **Beads and Baubles:** Emblazon entire titles in micro beads or choose a few baubles to dot title letters.
- **Glitter:** With the help of double-sided tape, entire titles can shimmer with glitter. For more understated bling, add a layer of glitter glue to letters.
- **Gloss:** Glaze letters with clear gloss medium or heat emboss for a shiny varnish.
- **Dimension:** Whether you use foam adhesive or create the illusion of dimension with layered mats or letter shadows, letters that appear to jump off the page command attention.

One day last Fall, Robby stayed home from school with tummy troubles. Hmmmm.... was he truly sick? He had been, but once he felt a touch better, he so wanted to play outside. I let him & then he felt bad again!

2005

Home Sick?

Shannon Taylor, Bristol, Tennessee

These acrylic letters clearly make a statement. Their transparency is symbolic of a mother questioning the seriousness of her son's ailment, but their slightly milky tone also is significant of an ailing boy. The peekaboo effect of the letters is contained within a solid, bold, black outline created with paint. The two lettering styles, both basic and clean, impart a feeling of stability.

Supplies: Patterned paper (A2Z Essentials, Scenic Route Paper Co.); buttons (Autumn Leaves); crayons; rub-on letters (Making Memories); clear letters (Heidi Swapp); acrylic paint; pen; cardstock

You Are
So Beautiful

Barb Hogan, Cincinnati, Ohio

Handwritten titles are so precious. Handwritten anything is a wonderful addition to a scrapbook page because it adds such a personal touch. On this page, the title, borrowed from a Joe Cocker song, anchors the bottom left of the page while sweetly framing a support photo. Beautiful script lettering is enhanced by doodles that extend from the letters like flowering vines.

Supplies: Patterned paper (BasicGrey); glitter dimensional paint (Ranger); corner rounder; pen; cardstock

LITTLE GIRLS ARE *heaven's flowers*

Big, impressive handwritten titles are an easy way to decorate a page. Here, the title stretches vertically from bottom to top, filling up a gutter of space between the focal photo and a ladder of supporting images. This title was created with brush and calligraphy pens. After the title was written in pencil (pencil marks erase *much* easier than pen; trust us!), it was outlined in black, colored in with purple and then detailed with white. If you balk at creating a handwritten title because you hate your handwriting, simply use a lettering template. No one will be the wiser.

Supplies: Patterned paper (Daisy D's, Making Memories); acrylic flowers, brads (Queen & Co.); rub-ons (Fiskars); glitter (Ranger); pen; cardstock

Beauty

Vicki Boutin, Burlington, Ontario, Canada

Within the image: Love, happy, Laughter, Mentor, tenderness, Respect, honor, Faith, Bonded together Forever

Bonded
Together Forever

Heather Preckel, Swannanoa, North Carolina

So you don't want to add handwriting to a layout because, if you make a mistake while writing, you'll ruin the layout. Understood, but that won't happen if you create your handwritten title on a separate sheet of paper, cut it out and adhere it to your layout. This title takes advantage of the high contrast between black and white. The words get extra emphasis with sweet doodles and double lines.

Supplies: Patterned paper (A2Z Essentials); buttons (Heidi Grace Designs); ribbon (May Arts); decorative tape (7 Gypsies); brads, silk flowers (Bazzill); dye ink; adhesive foam; pen; cardstock

Kersten is a daughter of our good friends, Bob and Aime. She is a lovely little girl, and despite the four year age difference between the two, is a wonderful friend to Reagan. They have sleepovers and play dates.

Every time I see them together, I can't help but see the similarities in their appearance. They could be sisters. The same fine curly blonde locks. The same fair skin. The same long narrow face. The same cute button nose.

But they are not sisters...but they are friends and that makes me happy.

They Could be Sisters

You can include your handwriting and mask its imperfections by stitching over it. Simply write out the title in pencil, pierce holes to use as stitching guides, thread the needle and stitch with a simple straight stitch. This title occupies a clean block of white space, giving it room to be admired as well as incorporating a clean color contrast. The purple thread also enhances the similar accent color found in the paper flowers and patterned paper.

Supplies: Patterned paper (My Mind's Eye); rub-ons (BasicGrey); brads, plastic flowers (Queen & Co.); die-cut flowers, micro beads (Provo Craft); embroidery floss; dimensional adhesive; cardstock; Weathered Fence font (Two Peas in a Bucket)

Sisters

Amber Baley, Waupun, Wisconsin

A Cell Phone

Amber Baley, Waupun, Wisconsin

This title invites a reader to linger. The divided letters of the title cause the reader to pay a bit more attention to the message and charm the reader by mimicking the keypad of a cell phone. White stitches adhere letters that were individually cut from a transparency sheet and add a bit of pop against a navy background and otherwise muted letters.

Supplies: Patterned paper (Chatterbox); transparency (K & Company); buttons (7 Gypsies); embroidery floss; pen; cardstock; Weathered Fence font (Two Peas in a Bucket)

3 Months

Jessica Sprague, Cary, North Carolina

This title's message is simple, but the technique hints at something more symbolic. A white number sticker was double-matted with patterned paper and blue cardstock, then stitched to the background. The stripes and stitch marks create a sense of the quirky movement of rapid growth. Stitching continues throughout the layout to secure the photo collage, which is a great way to show the range of adorable expressions a baby can have.

Supplies: Patterned paper (Cosmo Cricket); chipboard shapes (Li'l Davis Designs); fabric letters (Scrapworks); number sticker (American Crafts); thread; cardstock

This hand-sewn title looks anything but rustic. In fact, it's playful and chic with its mix of spunky plaid and vibrant color accents. The supersized fabric "K" creates a bold statement. It also helps to balance the page, draws in and guides the eye and anchors the photo. The cursive letters soften the large, blocky design.

Supplies: Fabric (Wal-Mart); embroidery floss; brads (Bazzill); adhesive foam; pen; cardstock

Kiersten

Heather Preckel
Swannanoa, North Carolina

Look at You

Vicki Boutin, Burlington, Ontario, Canada

The vertical, zigzag letters of this title add unquestionable energy to the page. Letters were traced from a template, cut out of patterned paper and then matted with a cool blue using foam adhesive. This results in dimension and a punch of color. The negative spaces from the cut-out letters were detailed with pen for definition.

Supplies: Patterned paper (Heidi Grace Designs, Scenic Route Paper Co.); chipboard flower, letter template, rub-ons (Fiskars); stamps (Gel-a-tins); rhinestones (source unknown); adhesive foam; pencil; pen; cardstock

I Heart You

Becky Fleck, Columbus, Montana

How could you not "heart" this layout? The heart theme pops up everywhere. It was inspired from the heart-shaped rock collection in the photo. The word "heart" and a heart shape appear in the title. The word is emphasized via color and draws the eye directly to the heart in the photo. Look closely and you'll see a stitched heart hugging the heart made of rocks in the photo and extending onto the background of the layout.

Supplies: Patterned paper (Chatterbox, Rhonna Designs); chipboard letters (Scenic Route Paper Co.); chipboard accents (Heidi Swapp); rub-ons (Scrapworks); decorative scissors; dye ink; thread; cardstock

MOMENTS · MOMENTS · MOMENTS · MOMENTS · MOMENTS

Fall is my favorite time of the year! I love all the changing colors; the crunchy leaves; playing in the leaves; Halloween; trick or treating; walks on the Parkway; fall festivals; the perfect weather; there is just nothing I don't love about this time of the year! Fall 2005

CHAPTER 2 Thinking Outside the Journaling Box

Journaling is absolutely integral to a scrapbook page. Without it, pages amount to a beautifully framed photo. For some scrapbook pages, journaling is unnecessary, but when there is a story behind a photo, journaling must present itself. Otherwise, the memory is lost. And you've spent too much time and had too much fun for *that* to happen.

Don't pigeonhole journaling as a lame and tedious assignment; journaling is fun (yes, we said it, fun!) and exists in many forms. Journaling can be extensive. Or, it can be short and caption-like. Journaling can live on a page in plain view, or it can be tucked and hidden away, discreetly, showing itself only to the most dedicated scrapbook-page reader. It can overlay photos and run along page edges. It can bounce along a page as a collection of descriptives and spring forth from design elements.

When designing a piece of journaling, try to avoid the "journaling block" mindset. That frame of mind categorizes journaling as something boxy and ancillary that just needs to be included on the page. The key is integrating it with the design and photos, not simply including it. Words can be highlighted, fonts can be mixed, media can be mixed, words can come to life.

The ideas that stretch out on the following pages will show you how to personify pages with words. Now, flip the page, look at your own journaled pages and tell them to "get a life."

Sometimes

Amber Baley, Waupun, Wisconsin

This bubbly, airy, imperfect cursive text leaves the reader with a sense of wistful hope. Like the image of the buoyant young girl, the text scampers across the page with carefree innocence. If creating a large text block with stickers seems a recipe for disaster ("Oops, I ran out of room!" or "Shoot! I misspelled 'and.'" or "Geez! I ran out of stickers!"), experiment on a sheet of wax paper first. The stickers will easily remove from the wax sheet after you evaluate how much space you need, if you have enough stickers, can spell correctly, etc., etc.

Supplies: Patterned paper (Chatterbox); die-cut letters (Provo Craft); buckles (Queen & Co.); fabric (source unknown); thread; cardstock; Suzie's font (Internet download)

Using mini alphabet stamps to create journaling can be time-consuming, but it looks so darn cute! The trick to accomplishing it while maintaining an air of sanity is to keep the journaling short and sweet (or, use the stamps to highlight key words of a journaling block). Also, forget perfection. By all means, spell everything correctly and follow some grammar rules, but don't fret about making sure everything is perfectly straight and spaced. These striking white journaling captions create a superb contrast against the bold black and pink background. They also keep the reader's eye on the photos.

Supplies: Patterned paper (A2Z Essentials); letter stamps (Technique Tuesday); beads, brads, flowers (Queen & Co.); dye ink; pen; cardstock

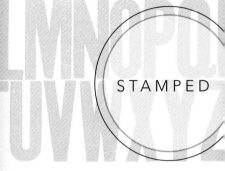

All Girl

Heather Preckel
Swannanoa, North Carolina

Venezia

Barb Hogan, Cincinnati, Ohio

This stamped body of text carries a vintage feel throughout the page. The distressed texture of the ink matches the tactile feel of the antique façade of Venice, Italy. Words are brought to the reader's attention via capitalization. Stamping the words directly onto an open area of the photo helps draw the eye and adds a sense of whimsy to the layout.

Supplies: Patterned paper (7 Gypsies, Autumn Leaves, Provo Craft); paper flowers (Prima); silk flowers (Michaels); buttons; book plate (Go West Studios); rubber stamps (Hero Arts, Making Memories); distress ink; acrylic paint

Content drives design. This is the graphic designer's mantra, and it means the text and photos establish the mood that the design in turn communicates. This silly photo calls for a design that is fun and playful, hence the dripping polka dots and funky curves. The curves found in the lettering style of this stamp set match the curve of the path the stamped text follows. The swirls create an unexpected home for the journaling, so they immediately grab attention while directing the eye to the photo.

Supplies: Patterned paper, chipboard letters (Scenic Route Paper Co.); letter stamps (Hero Arts); stamping ink; circle punch; brads; cardstock

This Face

Greta Hammond, Goshen, Indiana

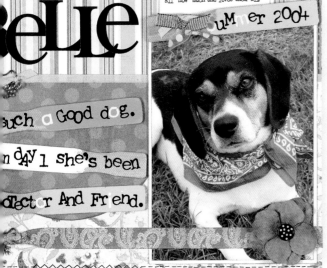

RUB-ONS

Belle

Kathy Fesmire, Athens, Tennessee

This lettering style is playful because this layout calls for nuthin' too fancy. The craft sticks were dipped in paint for no other reason than "it looks cool." They bring dimension to the page while echoing the color scheme. Rub-ons were used to add journaling to the sticks, with an odd highlighted letter here and there for good measure. Behind the photo is more journaling that waxes poetic about this family's furry friend.

Supplies: Patterned paper (My Mind's Eye); rub-on letters (Making Memories); letter stickers, rub-on accents (Doodlebug Designs); silk flowers (Teters); craft sticks; brad (Queen & Co.); binder clips; decoupage medium; acrylic paint; dye ink; ribbon (Offray); charm (source unknown)

It was just an inexpensive costume that I found in a hand-me-down box, but once the makeup was added, my girl was transformed into an adorable puppy. I love how this picture totally captures her playing the part, tongue hanging out and panting like the dog she has become.

Halloween '05

COMPUTER

puppy

Puppy

Amber Baley, Waupun, Wisconsin

An otherwise dense paragraph becomes very legible once cut into strips. Cutting a journaling block into strips sets loose some creative juice, allowing the lines to slant, tilt and stretch across the background. These strips, with their black text atop a subtle abstract pattern on a white backdrop, also subdue a somewhat busy pink background. The pleated paper border was created by accordion folding a strip of paper. Inside the black envelope lie more adorable photos.

Supplies: Patterned paper (7 Gypsies); plastic letters (Heidi Swapp); envelope (Li'l Davis Designs); buttons; embroidery floss; photo corners; thread; cardstock

Fall

Heather Preckel
Swannanoa, North Carolina

This journaling has a Magnetic Poetry® feel to it—as if you could paw at the individual words and rearrange them to your heart's content. The basic typewriter font is perfect for a fall page, with its no-muss, no-fuss feel. As the text wraps around the focal point within the photo, it encourages the reader to spend some time with the bordering photo collage, each piece of it a visual to support the rich written details.

Supplies: Cardstock; rubber stamp (Hero Arts); dye ink; rickrack (Offray); metal leaves (Nunn Design); brads; adhesive foam; pen; Antique Typewriter font (Internet download)

White, computer-printed text! How is it possible? It's really nothing dramatic—simply opt to reverse print your text onto white cardstock. These strips of text are an effective contrast against the playful polka-dot pattern. They overlap an encapsulating blue ring, which helps enhance the photo by highlighting the boy's eyes. It also provides a curving baseline for the reflective title.

Supplies: Patterned paper (American Crafts); die-cut letters (QuicKutz); circle sticker (Memories Complete); large paper clip (Bazzill); flowers (Doodlebug Designs); brad; tag (Making Memories); fabric tab (Scrapworks); embroidery floss; cardstock; Sans Serif font (Microsoft)

If I Only Knew

Linda Harrison, Sarasota, Florida

Street Savvy

Kathy Fesmire, Athens, Tennessee

The scripty font used for the concise journaling strips show a sophistication that perfectly complements the title. The phrases were composed using parallel construction, which heightens the effect of the stacked horizontal strips. These paper strips echo the colors of the photos and provide a unifying element for strips in the title and the striped patterned paper.

Supplies: Patterned paper (BasicGrey); chipboard letters (Heidi Swapp); letter brads (Paper Studio); ribbons (Offray); silk flowers (Teters); stamping ink; paper clips; cardstock

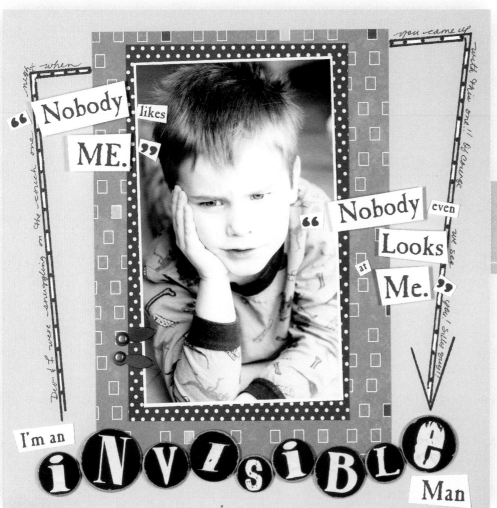

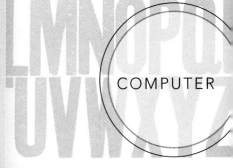

The strong language of this journaling, which is the poignant dialogue of a young son, deserves to be front and center. It frames the subject's face like floating thought bubbles found in the Sunday funnies. Along with the title, the journaling forms a visual triangle that wraps around the photo. Handwritten journaling careens around an extended framing accent.

Supplies: Patterned paper (A2Z Essentials); chipboard letters (Li'l Davis Designs); brads; photo turns; pen; cardstock

I'm an
Invisible Man

Vicki Boutin
Burlington, Ontario, Canada

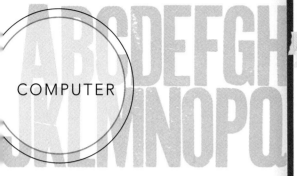

Watch the ocean for a while. Listen to the waves crash. Swim.

taking on the ocean

laughing and loving every

moment of it

just a little boy in a hat

tumbling and

june 8 2005

me and the sea

Design Do's and Don'ts

Break these design rules if you dare—you are, after all, master of your scrapbook domain. But these are a few of the general guidelines graphic designers follow:

DO

- limit each layout to three different fonts. If you must add more variety, vary point size or color.

- design vertical type by turning an entire word sideways rather than stacking the letters—it's easier to read.

DON'T

- distort or condense fonts, even though many software programs will let you.

- design large blocks of text using all italics, all block capital letters, or right-aligned text. It is difficult to read.

Me and the Sea

Joanna Bolick, Fletcher, North Carolina

What looks like a lost hat blowing across the water is actually a hat on top of a swimming boy, his body hidden by the water. To keep in line with the beach theme, this text flows across the page in waves. The faux-stitched waves were created with image editing software, and the text was added with the "text on a path" tool. The lowercase letters and fragmented sentences add to the childlike feel of the page.

Supplies: Patterned paper (KI Memories); brush stitch (Adobe); cardstock; Lainie Day SH, Minion fonts (Internet downloads)

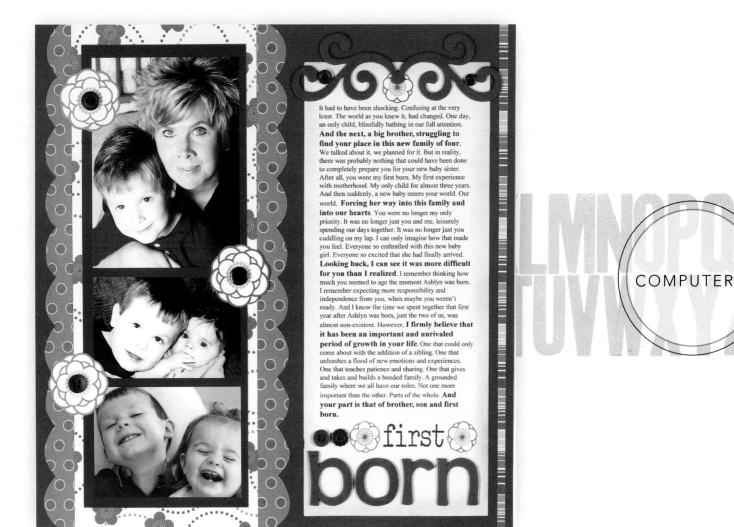

This journaling is heartfelt and a focal point of the page. Therefore, it was a wise decision to print it in a very simple and readable font and point size. The alignment is justified left for a clean feel. In five instances, text is highlighted with a slightly larger point size and heavy bolding. This technique breaks up the long text block into digestible chunks.

Supplies: Patterned paper, chipboard letters (Scenic Route Paper Co.); letter rub-ons (Imagination Project); chipboard accent (Fancy Pants Designs); acrylic paint; buttons (Autumn Leaves); cardstock

First Born

Greta Hammond, Goshen, Indiana

Big Bro

Becky Fleck
Columbus, Montana

A passage from a favorite children's book expresses the perfect sentiment for this page about brotherly love. The text was printed in a font that boasts wide, curved letters, a text style typical of children's books. The ragged alignment of the text block allows it to frolic about while alleviating any balance and value problems caused by short lines of text.

Supplies: Patterned paper, chipboard letters (Scenic Route Paper Co.); rub-on letters (Making Memories); chipboard shapes (Bazzill); ribbon (Shoebox Trims); brads; Broadsheet font (Internet download)

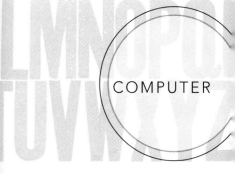

Like a family portrait hung above the fireplace to be admired by all, this journaling exists as a framed character study on this page. This layout, with its idyllic feel, is the perfect home for a formal journaling accent. The photos and journaling work excellently together. The journaling brims with detail about this boy's love of animals, while each visual image supports it.

Supplies: Patterned paper (A2Z Essentials, Making Memories); chipboard letters (Heidi Swapp); chipboard shapes (We R Memory Keepers); rub-on letters (Making Memories); rub-on accents (Autumn Leaves, BasicGrey); bookplate (BasicGrey); acrylic paint; cardstock

All Creatures

Greta Hammond, Goshen, Indiana

Legacy

Barb Hogan, Cincinnati, Ohio

The ornamental type styling of this journaling font conjures images of fair maidens waiting for their Prince Charming, which makes it perfect to describe the honor of receiving a fairytale ring. The journaling, on this all-digital layout, begins like a fairytale with a fancy drop cap to denote the start of the text.

Supplies: Image editing software (Adobe); digital elements (Kathy Moore, Shabby Princess, Something Blue Studios)

We Love to Pose

Shannon Taylor, Bristol, Tennessee

When it comes to journaling, computers rock. Computer-printed journaling exits the printer in pristine fashion, with perfectly spaced letters and words, even alignment, and exquisitely spell-checked text (you do spell-check, don't you?). Here, computer-printed journaling is taken to another level. In fact, it hits the sky. Well, it replaces the sky. In this photo, the sky originally appeared bright and overexposed. The color was changed to match the background and then filled in with journaling.

Supplies: Patterned paper, ribbon (We R Memory Keepers); chipboard shapes (Fancy Pants Designs); letter stickers (EK Success); adhesive foam; embroidery floss; stamping ink; cardstock

My Mentor, My Friend

Jessica Sprague, Cary, North Carolina

At first glance, this layout does not appear to be text heavy, but it is. Two-thirds of the journaling sweetly hides behind the photo, allowing the exposed layout to breathe with white space. A pull quote works to break up the text. Pull quotes are used in newspapers and magazines to emphasize a strong quote. The quotes are literally pulled from the text and highlighted via size and text of a heavier weight (and sometimes a different color).

Supplies: Patterned paper, page tacks (Chatterbox); die-cut letters (QuicKutz); corner rounder; circle punch; cardstock

Licensed to Fish

Becky Fleck, Columbus, Montana

The conversational tone of this journaling is peppered with dialogue and captures the true vernacular of the storyteller. The journaling is lengthy, so to compensate it lies under a transparency on which a photo was printed. Once the transparency is pulled up to reveal the story, the reader's eye is pleased with very clean body text that has been broken into digestible chunks of information.

Supplies: Patterned paper, letter stickers (American Crafts); index tabs (Heidi Swapp); sticker tab (My Mind's Eye); magnetic snap (BasicGrey); transparency; thread; medallion from keychain (artist's own souvenir); cardstock; Avant Garde, Carpenter fonts (Internet download)

" But Mom,

I said, Why?

Why? "

good question?

We have officially entered the stage of "further explanation"! (Robby at three)

Good Question

Linda Harrison, Sarasota, Florida

There are few creatures more curious in this world than a three-year-old child. They can walk, have learned to talk and, suddenly, everything is a mystery, and parents hold the key to unlock all answers. This layout captures the tenacity of the young and quizzical. The journaling font chosen includes italicized letters within the words that ignite images of a vowel-stretching voice—"But...whyyyyyyyy?"

Supplies: Patterned paper (American Crafts); die-cut shapes (QuicKutz); plastic embellishments (Heidi Swapp); cardstock; Will & Grace font (Dafont)

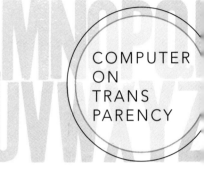

A singular circle of text marking the milestone of a baby's first birthday effortlessly acts as part of the title. The photo benefits from a vintage feel courtesy of a filter found in image editing software. This vintage effect paved the way for an old-fashioned design theme. The journaling was printed onto a transparency twice and layered to help darken the text.

Supplies: Patterned paper (7 Gypsies, Daisy D's, Melissa Frances); transparencies (Hambly Studios); rub-ons (Creative Imaginations, KI Memories); stickers (7 Gypsies, Making Memories); ribbon stamp (Hero Arts); solvent ink; digital photo treatment (Internet download)

1 Year Old

Joanna Bolick, Fletcher, North Carolina

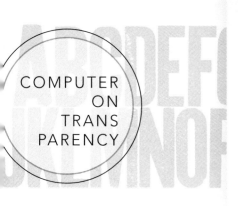

A New Do

Amber Baley, Waupun, Wisconsin

This journaling frames the layout and exists as part of a series of frames (patterned-paper edge and stitching). The journaling was printed onto a transparency and mounted to the page background with eyelets. The photos, the harlequin pattern, flower and ribbon accents were then mounted on top.

Supplies: Patterned paper (Fancy Pants Designs, My Mind's Eye); transparency (Grafix); ribbon (Offray); rhinestones (Beadery); die-cut flowers (Provo Craft); button; embroidery floss; eyelets; stamping ink; thread; twine; cardstock

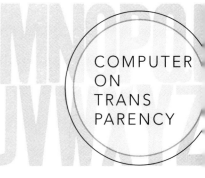

Huggles

Linda Harrison, Sarasota, Florida

A font that bounces and squishes is perfect for a page about innocent hugs, or "huggles." This playful font skips across columns of vibrant color. The journaling was trimmed into strips, which allowed for large, airy gaps of space between the lines of text. The transparency strips are adhered to the background with black decorative brads that blend into the background with ease.

Supplies: Transparency; die-cut letters (QuicKutz); rickrack; brads, tags (Making Memories); flowers, buttons (Doodlebug Designs); embroidery floss; cardstock; Shop-a-Holic font (Scrapsupply)

Telling the Story

Use these tips to encourage the words to stream upon the page.

- Use the five senses. Think of your memory in terms of touch, taste, smell, sight and sound.

- Free-associate. Meditate on your photos and write down any words that are conjured.

- Create a story arc. Think of your memory as if it were a story. What had to happen to reach the turning point? How was it resolved?

- Write a letter. Placing your memory inside a trusted framework can ease the stress involved.

- Tell someone. Talk to someone about the memory; take notes.

- Answer the five Ws and an H—who, what, where, when, why and how.

ABCDEFGHIJKLMNOPQRSTUVWXYZ

COMPUTER
ON
TRANS
PARENCY

1 #1 Fear

Jessica Sprague, Cary, North Carolina

The journaling is integrated into this design so the concept of fear is dramatized. The overall design takes a print-media approach. The symbolic imagery, hard defining lines of the photos, the black-and-white photography, the red flourishes that dip in and out of the focal photo are all nods to iconic print advertising. The text was printed onto a transparency in black to result in a strong contrast against the brick background. Key words are highlighted throughout the text in a dark and gritty font.

Supplies: Patterned paper, ribbon (American Crafts); rub-ons (7 Gypsies, Heidi Swapp); vellum adhesive; cardstock; digital brushes (artist's own design); Asman font (Dafont); Century Gothic font (Microsoft)

Beauty

Kathy Fesmire, Athens, Tennessee

Printing text on vellum creates easy elegance on pages. The murky transparency of the vellum hints at the pattern beneath.Streaks of paint were used to highlight words, and the blue also unifies the bold blue title. Once printed, the vellum was torn and the edges rolled to mimic the ocean waves.

Supplies: Patterned paper (My Mind's Eye); vellum (Grafix); rub-ons (K & Company); ribbon (Offray); die-cut letters (Provo Craft); acrylic paint; adhesive foam; embroidery floss; flower (artist's own design); stamping ink; cardstock

COMPUTER ON VELLUM

Peaceful

Greta Hammond, Goshen, Indiana

Journaling. It's a great place to get reflective. This journaling espouses the fact that a parent should not take an elusive peaceful moment for granted. The distressed typewriter font matches the layout's casual feel as well. Printing journaling on vellum lets you unobtrusively incorporate it into the design. Here, the journaling overlaps an empty spot on the photo without covering it completely.

Supplies: Patterned paper, bookplate (Scenic Route Paper Co.); vellum; chipboard letters (Heidi Swapp); rub-ons (Fancy Pants Designs); buttons (Autumn Leaves); brads; dye ink; embroidery floss; rickrack; cardstock

Maggiano's
Little Italy

Sharon Laakkonen, Superior, Wisconsin

So, your penmanship is neat enough; it's the fact that you tend to write uphill that makes you hesitant to include handwritten journaling on your pages? That problem can be somewhat alleviated if you trim your journaling block into strips. This technique also allows you to easily tailor the line length to the design. In this layout, the horizontal lines of the journaling strips contrast against the vertical lines of the patterned background. Under the bottom photo, short descriptives create a detail-rich photo caption while mimicking the bricks in the photo.

Supplies: Patterned paper (Prima); buttons (Autumn Leaves, Wal-Mart); dye ink; paper take-out bag (restaurant souvenir); corner rounder; thread; pen; cardstock

In addition to a collection of cropped index prints, four blocks of handwritten text frame this photo. The journaling is Mom's handwritten letter of love to her daughter—it is a priceless gift for a daughter to cherish forever. In regard to handwritten text, having a pen to complement your writing style will make all the difference in the world. Whether fine-tipped, ballpoint or felt-tipped, experiment with different pens until you find one that rests nicely in your hand.

Supplies: Patterned paper (My Mind's Eye); flower punches (EK Success); buttons (Junkitz); brads (American Crafts); ribbon, rickrack (May Arts); adhesive foam; pen; cardstock

Kiersten

Heather Preckel, Swannanoa, North Carolina

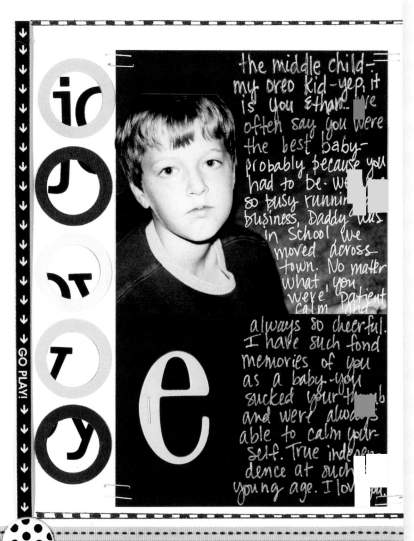

Joy

Kim Kesti, Phoenix, Arizona

This column of handwritten journaling flows seamlessly from the cardstock background to the photo and then back to the cardstock background. The text-heavy page is an appreciative message from a mother to a son, a message that might have gone unknown had it not been for Mom's thoughtfulness to put it on a page.

Supplies: Cardstock; letter stickers (American Crafts); plastic letter (Heidi Swapp); sticker strip (Provo Craft); ribbon (BasicGrey); large brad (Bazzill); circle punch; staples; pen

I have to admit that I **often did not** like having to pose for Dad. It seemed like he always had me facing to the sun so I **couldn't** see! It totally hurt my eyes. But now, I'm **grateful!** We have some great photos of me & my siblings. It's hard to believe that me, Heidi & Andy were ever this young!! Thanks Dad ♥

Shannon 7 yrs old

Heidi 3 years old

Andy less than a year

While it's never a bad idea to include personal handwriting on a page, certain page topics naturally will lend themselves to the style of your penmanship. On this layout, the mood is casual and laid-back, making it the perfect canvas for the artist's relaxed writing style. Words are highlighted in the artist's own handwritten block lettering, which she also colored in for emphasis. The handwriting is carried through the page via concho-encased photo captions.

Supplies: Patterned paper, metal tags (Daisy D's); fabrics (Junkitz); buttons (Junkitz, Making Memories); clip (Pebbles); embroidery floss; pen

Siblings

Shannon Taylor, Bristol, Tennessee

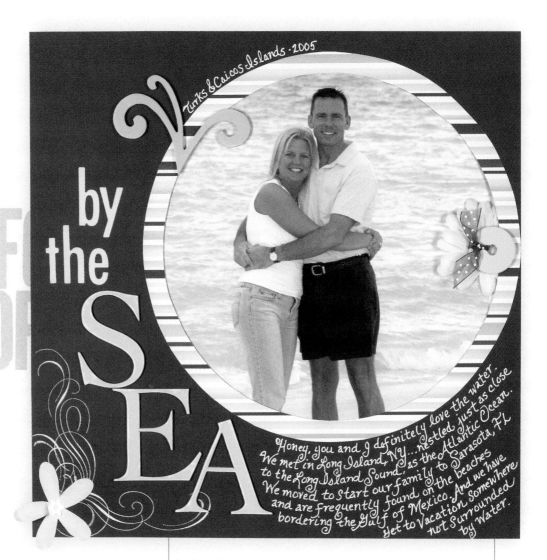

Turks & Caicos Islands · 2005

by
the
SEA

Honey, you and I definitely love the water.
We met in Long Island, NY...nestled just as close
to the Long Island Sound, as the Atlantic Ocean.
We moved to start our family to Sarasota, FL
and are frequently found on the beaches
bordering the Gulf of Mexico. And we have
yet to vacation somewhere
not surrounded
by water.

By the Sea

Linda Harrison, Sarasota, Florida

The handwriting on this page is a scriptier, curvier version of the artist's regular, everyday handwriting. The swirliness matches the beach theme as it curves along the bottom edge of the photo. The circular crop of the photo is reminiscent of porthole windows common to cruise ships. The frothy white of the pen ink evokes cresting waves.

Supplies: Patterned paper (We R Memory Keepers); chipboard letters (Heidi Swapp); die-cut letters (QuicKutz); chipboard accent (Deluxe Designs); rub-on (BasicGrey); flower (Bazzill); ribbon (SEI); acrylic paint; circle cutter; pen; cardstock

The journaling on this page reads like an entry from a daily diary. The handwritten text on notebook patterned paper echoes that emotion. The reader instantly falls under the spell of the conversational tone, wondering if there could be a more perfect way to capture the feelings and reflections inspired by a single day.

Supplies: Patterned paper (Creative Imaginations, Heidi Grace Designs, Karen Foster Design, Making Memories); letter stickers (Making Memories); cardstock tab (Heidi Grace Designs); rub-ons (My Mind's Eye); pen; cardstock

Little One

Joanna Bolick, Fletcher, North Carolina

The handwritten journaling on the layout reads:

Kiersten is such a daddy's girl ~ I love the relationship they have and the special bond that they have that goes way beyond any words. I know it will be a special bond between them that will stand the test of time. They bring out the best in each other and have the best of times. Kiersten is one very lucky little girl to have such a daddy.

Kiersten and Daddy

forever together

May 2006

Kiersten and Daddy

Heather Preckel, Swannanoa, North Carolina

The journaling on this page is fully integrated into the design. The journaling certainly stands on its own, but it also exists as part of the pattern-blocked background design. When journaling on vellum, it is very easy for the ink to smudge. Always experiment with the pen first because some pens are better than others for writing on vellum.

Supplies: Vellum (American Crafts); ribbon (May Arts); brads, stickers (Bazzill);
buttons (Junkitz); pen; cardstock

The Wind in My Face

Sharon Laakkonen, Superior, Wisconsin

Like gusts of wind, the journaling blows across the top of this page. It serves as a wonderful border to the adorable wall of photos that stretches across the page. The handwritten journaling matches the handwritten element in the title. The rest of the title was cut from alphabet-patterned paper.

Supplies: Patterned paper (Imagination Project); letter paper (FontWerks); thread; pen; dye ink; cardstock

I Love You

Jessica Sprague, Cary, North Carolina

Does a more wonderful and unique bouquet of flowers exist for this little girl? Mom's handwriting runs up and down the stems of handcrafted flowers. Mom used a journaling template to create the curving stem lines that act as the perfect baseline for the text. Using your handwriting as a design element is a great way to mask any imperfections.

Supplies: Patterned paper (Scenic Route Paper Co.); chipboard letters, decorative tape (Heidi Swapp); date stamp (Technique Tuesday); stamping ink; adhesive foam; journaling template (Chatterbox); pen; cardstock

Handwriter's Anonymous

Follow this 8-step program for including your handwriting on page layouts:

1. Love your handwriting. Almost everyone criticizes their penmanship. Learn to love yours, scrawls and all.

2. Practice. The only way to improve your handwriting is to practice.

3. Find the right pen. Use a pen that complements your writing style.

4. Accept mistakes. They will happen; sigh and move on.

5. Keep it straight, if you want. Journaling templates can keep your hand on the straight and narrow.

6. Hide it. If you really hate your writing, simply hide it in an envelope or behind a photo.

7. Turn it into a font. Mix the personalized look of your handwriting with the convenience of your computer with vLetter software, www.vletter.com, which will create a font based on a handwriting sample.

8. Include it in small amounts. If you really, truly hate your writing, consider using it in small amounts, such as for captions.

The handwritten journaling meanders along this page just like an ice skater's tracks along a rink or frozen pond. This swirling line of bold purple creates definite movement and definite draw on this page while housing the title. The chosen accents and patterns have a similar curving quality.

Supplies: Patterned paper (Imagination Project); flowers (Prima); circle punch; beads; embroidery floss; dye ink; pen; cardstock

New Skates

**Sharon Laakkonen
Superior, Wisconsin**

Supplies: Patterned paper (Chatterbox); gaffer tape (7 Gypsies); transparency (Hambly Studios); chipboard letters (Li'l Davis Designs); charms (Nunn Design); ledger paper; ribbon (Strano); pen; cardstock

Addict

Kim Kesti, Phoenix, Arizona

Some people have "likes," while other, more passionate people have "addictions." This confessional begins with the title. The word "addict" contains an "i" in a different style and size to emphasize the subject's ownership of the habits. A string of charms guides the eye to the list-style journaling, which is an efficient way to include lots of detail on a page. The handwritten list on notebook paper is another effective way to get the point across. Black-and-white photos add to an almost clinical feel.

Flowers of the **Meadow**

Barb Hogan, Cincinnati, Ohio

Handwritten journaling on a digital scrapbook page...wait, how is that possible? There are a few ways to include personal handwriting on a digital scrapbook page (actually, you can use the following techniques to include handwriting on a traditional page as well). Software exists that will turn your handwriting into a font (see page 84 for more information). Or you can write out the journaling and scan it into your computer. Then import the image onto your digital scrapbook page.

Supplies: Image editing software (Adobe); digital elements (Shabby Princess)

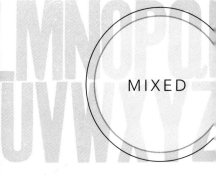

The journaling is a featured element on this page. It employs rub-ons, handwriting and chipboard lettering and rests on a playful yet inconspicuous patterned background. The rub-ons highlight key words while the handwriting creates the bulk of the body text.

Supplies: Patterned paper, chipboard letters (Scenic Route Paper Co.); chipboard shapes (Li'l Davis Designs); rub-ons (Sandylion, Scenic Route Paper Co.); beads (La De Da Designs); brads (Karen Foster Design); pen; cardstock

Play

Vicki Boutin
Burlington, Ontario, Canada

Peek-a-Boo!

Shannon Taylor, Bristol, Tennessee

Mixed-media and supersized letters that bounce along the page give this layout a very sing-songy feel. Big, black and bold lettering styles add a super dose of contrast while emphasizing key rhythmic words within the journaling. The words fall along lines that were machine stitched to the background. Curving pipe-cleaner accents resemble a music staff and keep the eye inside the design.

Supplies: Patterned paper, brads (Junkitz); chipboard letters (Heidi Swapp); letter stickers (American Crafts); rub-on letters (Making Memories); pipe cleaners; thread; pen

Heavy black stamped words give this journaling block a definite starting and stopping point. They also frame the elegant hand-written text inside and provide a solid contrast in type style. The journaling block extends left to also serve as a subtle photo mat, which is anchored by the title. The long horizontal bed of white adds a bit of breathing space since it sits atop an exciting and vertical background.

Supplies: Patterned paper, acrylic title (Heidi Grace Designs); rhinestone brads (Making Memories); stamps (Gel-a-tins); dye ink; circle cutter; pen; cardstock

I Love You

Vicki Boutin
Burlington, Ontario, Canada

lions & tigers & bears

Sometimes you're a **lion** sometimes you're a **tiger** and sometimes you're a **bear** to deal with! It is hard to believe you are almost six. You are starting to get a **mind** of your own and I see so much of **me** in **you**. There are days when you are telling me what to do and becoming frustrated when you don't get what you want. On those days, I wish you were still my little **baby** that just ate and slept. Then there are days I wouldn't **change** for the world, like this one at the Sculpture Park by Grammy's house. We had so much fun taking photos of you along side every sculpture, and this picture really shows the **sweet** **bear** I love to be with every day.

4-29-06

Journaling Treatments

Need a cool way to integrate your journaling into your scrapbook page? Look to the magazine experts. Make like an editor and use one of the following text treatments on your scrapbook page.

- **Caption Text:** These short chunks of text are great for capturing extra details or reinforcing a theme. They should accompany a visual element on the page, such as a photo or piece of memorabilia.

- **Sidebar:** These boxes of text contain ancillary information to accompany body text. They are usually full of facts, figures and otherwise helpful information that help give the story more context.

- **Pull Quote:** These are created from especially poignant quotes within the body text. The quote has so much impact, it is "pulled" from the text and emphasized. Pull quotes also break up long body text.

Lions & Tigers & Bears, Oh My!

Becky Fleck, Columbus, Montana

This page relies on the rule of thirds to produce a solid design. The journaling sits in the middle third, sandwiched inside two columns of patterns. The computer-printed text holds highlighted words, which were created with letter stamps. Tidy execution of this technique may require some trial and error, so it's best to experiment first. Type in the journaling and eyeball the space required for the stamped words. Print and hope for the best. If at first you don't succeed, try again (and perhaps again and again).

Supplies: Patterned paper, heart head pins (Heidi Grace Designs); chipboard letters (KI Memories); chipboard accents, rub-ons (BasicGrey); mini letter stamps (Pixie Press); tab (Heidi Swapp); dye ink; sewing machine; cardstock; Avant Garde font (Internet download)

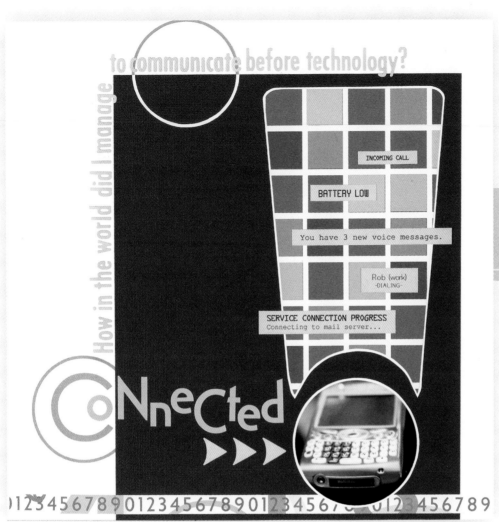

Connected

Linda Harrison, Sarasota, Florida

Journaling floats in techy fonts across this page. The simple phrases are just enough to make anyone living in this century think of a cell phone. The background of this page is quite literally punctuated with an exclamation point. Mosaic patterned paper used for the body of the exclamation was chosen for its likeness to a keypad.

Supplies: Patterned paper, letter stickers (Arctic Frog); die-cut letters and shapes (QuicKutz); circle punch; cardstock; Boring, Castorgate, Data Control fonts (Dafont); Courier New font (Microsoft)

Mommy's little darling

together

we love
to be
together

friends

o

we will grow
to be good
friends

good times

together
+
friends
=
good times

you & me • you & me • you & me • you & me

you & me

you & me • you & me

Designing Type with Style

Design your type. Integrate type into the design. Typography. These phrases and terms can sound a little high-brow and intimidating, but you don't need to be an expert in type to use it well. Common sense and a healthy awareness of your gut will suffice.

Picture yourself evaluating an almost-finished scrapbook page. You look closely at your page. Then you take a step back to view it from afar. Finally, you squint your eyes, blurring all definition, to survey the individual elements' weight values. Does it all feel right in your gut? Or is there something that, even for a second, keeps irking you?

When manipulating type, the slightest change can send a page soaring into the echelons of great page design. Make something bigger, emphasize a word through color, decrease the weight of a text block, switch a font to add more cohesiveness or increase the eclectic factor. Give a text block more air or condense the lines, adjust the proportion of the title to the subtitle, give a text background an entirely new texture. All these decisions can be based on your gut feeling about the way your page looks. You just need to learn what questions to ask yourself when thinking about type.

Typography is just words, and we use words every day. Just as you (hopefully) filter thoughts to verbally communicate with words, filter your thoughts to communicate with them visually. As we enter into this book's final chapter, prepare to learn a thing or two about marrying type with design. At the end of the journey, your type and design skills will be playing very well with each other.

Summer Day

Joanna Bolick, Fletcher, North Carolina

Get ready! Get set! Go...look at the photos! When you begin to design your scrapbook page, the photos should spark the inspiration. Look not only for colors, but textures, shapes and line quality. For example, in this layout, do you notice the use of strong horizontal lines in the background paper, title and journaling? They match the horizon, water and sand lines in the photo. Additional horizontal lines of text peek out from between the journaling strips.

Supplies: Patterned paper (Fancy Pants Designs, My Mind's Eye); acrylic stamps (Autumn Leaves); rubber stamps, velvet stickers (Making Memories); chipboard letters, decorative tape, plastic cards (Heidi Swapp); stickers (7 Gypsies); narrative tab (Creative Imaginations); rub-ons (7 Gypsies, BasicGrey, Creative Imaginations, Die Cuts With A View); acrylic paint; staples; cardstock

A bicycle
A hole
A fall
Crying
Grandparents
Leaving camp
Hospital
ER
Nurses
Doctors
Shots
Blue Sheet
Needle and thread
CAT Scan
Disney Channel
Back to camp
Stitched

When you're a parent, few things will send you to the land of near insanity more quickly than a trip to the emergency room. You're frantic with worry; thoughts are rampant and nearly impossible to collect. The journaling on this page captures that feeling of images and actions, occurring as if they were flash bulbs going off in your mind. The title is an obvious nod to the doctor's handiwork, while the blue background says only one thing: scrubs.

Stitched

Kathy Fesmire, Athens, Tennessee

Supplies: Patterned paper (BasicGrey, My Mind's Eye); rub-ons (EK Success); corner punch; circle punch; embroidery floss; notebook paper; pen; cardstock; Butterbrotpapier font (Internet download)

Good year! Robby seemed to enjoy it!

Football touchdown for mommy's birthday

"I love Laken" written on his hand   Signed DeAngelo Hall jersey for his birthday

Yugioh obsession   Super awesome grades   Big time buddy - Jamil Daggs

Amazing basketball defender   Yup, it was a good year!

3rd Grade

Robby Taylor - 2006

STICKERS

3rd Grade

Shannon Taylor, Bristol, Tennessee

The type on this page has a lot of jobs—it creates weight, adds balance, produces rhythm and echoes accent colors. The title gives the eye a nice yet unconventional starting point. It also creates rhythm on the page: What one shape repeats across this page? A block. The title fits inside an imaginary block shape, which is then repeated in the photo series. The "8" begins that photo series with a bang and pops the red within the grouping. Running the journaling strips across a busy alphabet-stickers background is a great way to subdue the chaos.

Supplies: Letter stickers (Making Memories); chipboard letters (Heidi Swapp); chipboard accents (Junkitz); number sticker (American Crafts); acrylic paint; textured paper (source unknown); cardstock

Not-Your-Typical
Gift Cards

Becky Fleck, Columbus, Montana

Word. These are like, totally rad! Pardon our teen speak, but the use of that casual phraseology spelled out in stickers makes these cards, like, awesome. The handmade cards show a great mix of patterns that are governed and smoothed by color and proportion, which also add some junk to this funk. The colors are super juicy and hip, and the combinations rely on contrast to make a statement. Each card comes complete with a supersized die-cut letter that corresponds to the first letter of each suhweet phrase. The cards fit inside a cute multicolored tin that's been secured by strips of patterned paper and a magnetic closure.

Supplies: Patterned paper, magnetic snap (BasicGrey); circle cutter; decorative scissors; dye ink; PermEnamel paint (Delta); envelopes (artist's own design); tin (Fossil)

STICKERS

Font-Tastic

Tired of restricting your designs to the same tried-and-true fonts available in your word processing program—the same fonts everybody else has? Download some fun new typefaces from scrapbooker-friendly Web sites, such as:

www.twopeasinabucket.com

www.scrapbook.com

www.fontdiner.com

www.dafont.com

97

Handcrafted
Handbag

Greta Hammond, Goshen, Indiana

Women learn early in life the importance of accessories. Many believe the mantra, "Go clearance on the clothes; go big on the accessories." This texture-rich and carefree purse is only a splurge in creativity. Wonderful descriptive-word journaling lines the perimeter of the purse, using velvet letter stickers. The mix of styles borders on eclectic, all of them just as fun and funky as the next.

Supplies: Wood purse (DecoArt); patterned paper, die-cut flowers, jewels (Provo Craft); velvet letters (Heidi Swapp, Making Memories); ribbon (Offray, Provo Craft); acrylic paint; cardstock

ACRYLIC

With a magnetic bulletin board *this* cool, your to-do (and maybe your to-don't) lists will never go unnoticed or be forgotten. Cut the metal to desired size (or have the home improvement store do it for you), sand and fold the edges under, about 3 inches. Cut paper to size and adhere to metal with decoupage medium. Allow to dry and apply two more coats of decoupage medium; allow coats to dry between applications. Embellish as desired. Finally, embellish a plastic clothespin magnet with flirty ribbons. This board benefits from a beautiful photo anchored by clear, oversized, acrylic letters.

Supplies: Patterned paper (Arctic Frog); acrylic letters (KI Memories); ribbon (Offray); acrylic paint; decoupage medium; flower (Teters); large clothes pin (source unknown); magnets; buttons; sheet metal (home improvement store)

Magnetizing
Magnetic Board

Kathy Fesmire, Athens, Tennessee

A IS FOR ADORABLE
B IS FOR BABY
C IS FOR CUDDLING
D IS FOR DADDY
E IS FOR ENDLESS LOVE
F IS FOR FOREVER
G is for Girl
H IS FOR HAPPY
I is FOR iRREPLACABLE
J IS FOR JOY
K IS FOR KIERStEN
L IS FOR LOVE
M IS FOR MIRACLE
N IS FOR NEW
O IS FOR OUR ANGEL
P IS FOR PRECIOUS
Q IS FOR QUIEt
R IS FOR RADIANt
S IS FOR SWEEt
T IS FOR TINY
U IS FOR UNIQUE
V IS FOR VERY SPECIAL
W IS FOR WONDER
X IS FOR XtRA SPECIAL
Y IS FOR YOU
Z IS FOR AMAZING

Kiersten ~ 2 weeks

baby girl

ALPHA PAPER

Alphabet-patterned paper is a natural choice for baby and kid scrapbook pages. Here the alphabet theme is carried through the journaling. This type of journaling is easy and effective with the letters making wonderful prompts. Before you know it, you have 26 cool details to add to your page. Also striking are the unexpected color scheme and letter quality. The gritty font and white-and-green combo result in a very artistic composition that is appropriate but not at all cutesy.

Supplies: Patterned paper (7 Gypsies); chipboard letters (Provo Craft); rub-ons (Making Memories); brad, flower (Bazzill); ribbon (May Arts); dye ink; pen; cardstock; Vintage font (Internet download)

Baby Girl

Heather Preckel
Swannanoa, North Carolina

You begged for the slip -n- slide "you saw on Cartoon Network" and, as usual, I caved. I really didn't think you would slide on it because when Alex and Grace had theirs out in the yard, you were too scared to

try. It was a sign that you watch way too much TV and it made me realize we need to spend more time outside just having fun. It has been one of the best "spoiled rotten kid" purchases I have made in a long time. It really shows how truly happy you are just to be outside having a good time.

June 10, 2006

H2OH!

Becky Fleck, Columbus, Montana

Oh! How cool is the word play on this page? The title captures the theme and the excitement of a slippery summer drenched in fun. The text integrates completely with this design. A curving line of bubbly patterned paper splits the entire page in half, but the split is most impressive on the letter "H" in the title. Here the line, in an above/below-the-water type of fashion, signals a color switch. The journaling nestles inside the recesses of the "H."

Supplies: Patterned paper (American Craft, Provo Craft, Scenic Route Paper Co.); jumbo chipboard letter (Rusty Pickle); chipboard number (BasicGrey); 3D gloss medium; acrylic paint

A playful border hugs this page with sweet detail. Text-patterned paper was trimmed and reassembled to create the border, but not before the edges were inked to add just a hint of dimension. Handwritten journaling strips add to the sense of movement and pixyish rub-ons balance the straightforward typewriter font in a delicate fashion. In the title, we find wonderful color unity that really ties the page together.

Supplies: Patterned paper (A2Z Essentials, Imagination Project); chipboard and rub-on letters (Imagination Project); cork flowers (Prima); buttons (Autumn Leaves); dye ink; thread; pen; cardstock

Sweet Love

Sharon Laakkonen
Superior, Wisconsin

Ever since you were a few months old, you have showed signs of great concentration. As you progressed through the months, the only thing that changed is *what* you were focused on. Toys and books and favorite activities changed with your age, but the way each thing kept your attention did not. You could play with your favorite toy for extended periods of time without needing any other stimulation whatsoever. Your attention-span seemed to be more mature than you.

For months, I started to get used to that focus of yours and take it for granted. You continued to be easily entertained and maintain a healthy curiosity. Lately, however, that concentration of yours has come to my attention again and I am really noticing how it is helping you learn and grow. Now that you are using that focus to write your name, complete connect-the-dots and solve simple problems, I am seeing that this quality of yours is something that will be able to take you far in what you want to do. I just want you to know that I recognize your capabilities and I will always be here to support you in wherever your focus may take you.   Robby 07.2006

Focused!

Linda Harrison, Sarasota, Florida

In this layout, a chaotic pattern is controlled inside a clean, graphic design. The theme of this layout is focus—concentration amidst distraction. Visually the idea is communicated by an effective use of paper that features a jumbled alphabet pattern. The pattern is locked inside a finite space, bordered by definite lines. The journaling text is clean and space is used deliberately to evoke a sense of calm. Sandwiching its tranquility between the patterned paper and a jumping title also lends credibility to the theme.

Supplies: Patterned paper, letter stickers (Arctic Frog); circle punch; cardstock; Times New Roman font (Microsoft)

Girly Girl

Greta Hammond, Goshen, Indiana

The collection of patterns, colors and accents on this page make it the epitome of feminine. The text-patterned paper is custom designed. Ubiquitous girly words were typed into two lines of text and then repeated. The words exist in various styles and shades of pink to create a tone-on-tone effect when printed on pink paper. The uniform text has a smaller point size and scaled back color creating a theme-appropriate pattern that is comfortable as a supporting page element yet not a wall flower.

Supplies: Patterned paper (Polar Bear Press); chipboard letters, flower (Heidi Swapp); rub-ons (Autumn Leaves, My Mind's Eye); brads (Making Memories); acrylic paint; photo corners; cardstock

Body Text Rules

- Consider 14-point type for journaling. It's big enough to be easy on the eyes without interfering with other page elements.

- Emphasize words within text via bold or italicized treatments. Or highlight words with color, size or a contrasting font style.

- For long pieces of body text, opt for serif fonts, which are generally easier to read. Save the use of decorative fonts, also known as display fonts, for titles or when adding emphasis to individual words.

- When colorizing text, readability is the highest priority. Opt for color combinations with high contrast and only use color with intent (to add emphasis, energy or enhance mood). Resist the urge to colorize delicate fonts; it will compromise their readability.

This Makes Me Happy

Amber Baley, Waupun, Wisconsin

The phrases that border this wall of photos were cut from text-patterned paper. In the scrapbook store, an entire sheet of this same paper might look too busy or energetic to use. On this page, the many vibrant colors and bold lettering styles would have been too busy and energetic if they had not been used strategically. Instead they add movement and context.

Supplies: Patterned paper–including letters (K & Company, Rocky Mountain Scrapbook Co.); chipboard accents (source unknown); thread; sandpaper

This page expresses the romantic notions of childhood—the delicate nature of a babe that a mother yearns to hold onto forever. The flower accent, which wonderfully anchors and connects the three close-up portraits, contains a heartfelt message that spirals from its center. Handwritten journaling occupies cream strips of paper that rest atop petals cut from script-patterned paper. These sophisticated patterns that show a mother's love coordinate well with the more playful patterns that hint at childhood innocence.

Dev

Vicki Boutin, Burlington, Ontario, Canada

Supplies: Patterned paper (Autumn Leaves, Imagination Project, Scenic Route Paper Co., SEI); stamps (Gel-a-tins); stamping ink; chipboard shape (Imagination Project); button; pen

One Lovely Box

Jessica Sprague, Cary, North Carolina

Thinking inside the box has its benefits too. Sometimes you want to have a place to hold onto the mementos or store your 12" x 12" layouts. Keepsake boxes are wonderful for that purpose. This beautiful box evolved from a plain kraft box. Text-patterned papers in the theme of love were decoupaged over the box. Bold cardstock paper strips create a grid to define and unify all the patterns. The words "love" and "bliss" are eye-catching for their distressed, romantic lettering styles.

Supplies: Patterned paper (7 Gypsies, Bo-Bunny Press, Creative Imaginations, Junkitz); letter and heart stickers (Bo-Bunny Press); heart coasters (Imagination Project); Velcro; ribbons (source unknown); cardstock; file box (source unknown)

This emotional page has a decidedly masculine feel. The theme is soft and sentimental, yet through the pattern choice (stripes and plaids), the color choice (neutrals and soft green) and the sparse embellishment, the look is slightly rugged. A strong photo is balanced by an equally strong title, that is just the slightest bit quirky. The subtitle finds a great home inside chipboard brackets. A strip of dictionary-patterned paper creates distinction and reinforces the theme.

Supplies: Patterned paper (Crate Paper); chipboard accents (Heidi Swapp); stickers (Making Memories); buttons (Junkitz); dye ink; pen; cardstock

Love

Heather Preckel
Swannanoa, North Carolina

What does it matter that most of the stuff you use to make your trains isn't actually a train? Not one bit, I say. Trucks, cars, dolls, trees, they all make it into the lineup at some point, although you do love the wheeled stuff best.

You are living proof that as long as you have the right sound effect going, and your imagination turned on full blast, anything on earth can be a train. Thanks for the reminder.

Everything
is a
TRAIN
(with the right sound effects)

Everything
Is a Train

Jessica Sprague, Cary, North Carolina

Letter stamps can go where your computer-printed fonts could never go. That's not exactly true, but if you're not a digital dynamo, creating text on a curve could be kinda hard. Here, "choo choo" is stamped repeatedly along a rainbow of curving patterned paper. The repetition creates a sense of propulsion while the curves take your eye for a ride.

Supplies: Patterned paper (KI Memories, Urban Lily); acetate letters (Heidi Swapp); letter stamps (My Sentiments Exactly); stamping ink; flower, brad (Doodlebug Designs); cardstock; Asman and Century Gothic fonts (Dafont)

Knowledge of Nature

Shannon Taylor, Bristol, Tennessee

All of the lettering styles on this page speak to masculinity and knowledge. The chipboard letters that form the title lend an outdoorsy, homemade feel to the page while the journaling font is casual but full of endearment. The title for the hidden journaling block, with its architectural styling, shows pillars of strength.

Supplies: Patterned paper (Karen Foster Design); chipboard letters (Li'l Davis Designs); corrugated box; ribbon (Offray); acrylic paint; rubber stamps (Plaid, Stampa Rosa); number accents (Making Memories); epoxy charm (EK Success); paper flowers (Creative Paper Co.); Minya font (Internet download)

Wowsers
Wall Hanger

Vicki Boutin, Burlington, Ontario, Canada

Homemade wall hangers are a wonderful way to show a little love for your kids while expressing an appreciation and understanding of their style. This hanging is exemplary of a fun and spunky gal. The supersized chipboard monogram is the perfect backdrop for her name, spelled in spicy-styled rub-ons. The singular burst of orange makes a definite statement. It adds needed visual weight to contrast the bed of off-kilter blocks of fun and feminine patterned papers.

Supplies: Patterned paper (Heidi Grace Designs, Making Memories); chipboard flower, ribbon (Heidi Grace Designs); chipboard letter (BasicGrey); rub-ons (Imagination Project); rhinestones; button; hanging plaque (source unknown)

CHIPBOARD

A Funky
Fatherly Card

Barb Hogan, Cincinnati, Ohio

Pink–what a masculine color! Actually, we all know that pink is typically woman's turf, but here it works, adding unexpected zing to this masculine card. On the one hand, there are the stenciled letters that are very masculine. Those, coupled with the large chipboard letters with inky edges say, "Dad, you are a pillar of strength and stability." Incorporate the traditional male patterns of stripes and argyle in juicy color combos, and we see that Dad also has a warm and playful heart. And just to add a bit more zip, flip the letters around to uncover a special, hidden message.

Supplies: Patterned paper (American Crafts); chipboard and rub-on letters, decorative tape (Imagination Project); acrylic paint; brads; pigment ink; Kraft cardstock; pen

Dreamy Signage

Linda Harrison, Sarasota, Florida

How could you not be inspired by this sign, commanding that you not only dream, but "dream *big!*" This sign tricks us into thinking big, boundless thoughts full of whimsy with a seemingly unstructured design. Actually the design is well thought out. Start with the curves. First, we see them in the patterned paper, but suddenly they are everywhere, echoed in the scalloped edge of the green paper, the round buttons, the curvy shapes of the letters, the baseline of the word, "big," the flower accent, the polka-dot pattern. Contrast is a big kicker, too. Green and pink totally contrast, and that is only heightened by the strong contrast of the big, bold, black letters.

Supplies: wood plaque (Wal-Mart); patterned paper (Arctic Frog, Scenic Route Paper Co.); chipboard letters (BasicGrey); letter stickers (Arctic Frog); acrylic paint; buttons (Jo-Ann Stores); embroidery floss; ribbon (Offray); flowers (Michael Miller, Doodlebug Designs); pen; cardstock

Joy

Vicki Boutin, Burlington, Ontario, Canada

A truly joyful title bounces across the page. Three distinct but connected ideas stand behind this layout. Each is signaled by a sentence of handwritten journaling (a great personal touch to a mother-daughter layout), a chipboard word accent (a great way to reinforce the theme), and one of the title letters (a great way to add oomph to the title). A strip cut from text-patterned paper and a chipboard accent connect the three ideas.

Supplies: Patterned paper, chipboard letters, chipboard words (Scenic Route Paper Co.); chipboard shape (Imagination Project); heart charm (Jo-Ann Stores); brads (Karen Foster Design); rhinestones; pen; cardstock

A page about a little girl standing on the shoulders of the world needs to be bright and vibrant. This page showcases portraits of a beautiful two-year-old while expressing a mother's hope and wonder for the type of person she is becoming. Celebratory chipboard accents dot the page on the upper-left corner, giving the reader a wonderful welcome to the lovely portraits. A second chipboard accent reinforces the title.

Faces of Two

Greta Hammond, Goshen, Indiana

Supplies: Patterned paper, rub-ons (BasicGrey); rubber stamp (Hero Arts); chipboard accents (Fancy Pants Designs, Heidi Swapp); rickrack (source unknown); 3D gloss medium (Ranger); brads (Making Memories); photo corners (QuicKutz); cardstock

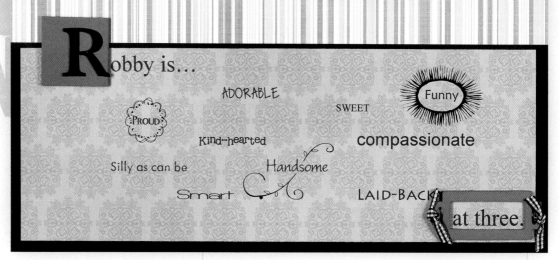

Robby Is...

Linda Harrison, Sarasota, Florida

Orange chipboard adds eye-catching contrast to this layout. Two dramatic letter "Rs" alert the reader that this page is about a boy named Robby. A similar orange tone is echoed in the singular strip of striped patterned paper that runs along the middle. Orange chipboard accents also create a visual triangle that guides the eye through the layout.

Supplies: Patterned paper (Chatterbox); large chipboard letter (Zsiage); small chipboard letter, tag (Making Memories); die-cut letters (QuicKutz); rub-ons (BasicGrey); ribbon (Offray); chipboard square (Bazzill); chipboard bookplate (source unknown); acrylic paint; cardstock

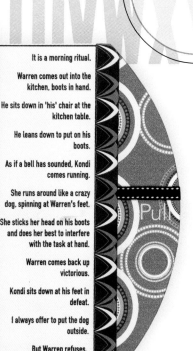

It is a morning ritual.

Warren comes out into the kitchen, boots in hand.

He sits down in 'his' chair at the kitchen table.

He leans down to put on his boots.

As if a bell has sounded, Kondi comes running.

She runs around like a crazy dog, spinning at Warren's feet.

She sticks her head on his boots and does her best to interfere with the task at hand.

Warren comes back up victorious.

Kondi sits down at his feet in defeat.

I always offer to put the dog outside.

But Warren refuses.

I think he likes it.

A Morning Ritual

Amber Baley, Waupun, Wisconsin

Gimme an "R" for "ruff!" Actually, gimme an "R" for "ritual," as this is the word the chipboard letter intends to highlight. This page expresses a morning routine so regular and adorable that it deserved to be commemorated. Journaling hidden behind the vertical wall of photos demands to be pulled out to explain the daily occurrence. The chipboard letter was covered in patterned paper and placed on a white background for maximum contrast.

Supplies: Patterned paper (Cherry Arte); chipboard letter (Li'l Davis Designs); rub-ons (Making Memories); ribbon (May Arts); stamping ink; corner rounder; cardstock; Fette Engschrift font (Internet download)

Type Terminology

- **Typeface** refers to a specific design of type, such as Times New Roman or Arial.

- **Serifs** are short strokes that extend from and to the individual letterforms. Fonts are either "serif" or "sans serif."

- **Ascenders** and **descenders** are the strokes of each letterform that either extend the x-height (ascender) or below the baseline (descender).

- **Leading** (pronounced "ledding") refers to the amount of vertical space between lines of type. Electronically, it is measured in point sizes, just like fonts.

- **Kerning** refers to the amount of horizontal space between letters. Condensed type has tight kerning.

You at 12

Kathy Fesmire, Athens, Tennessee

Everything about this page says, "pretty" and "feminine," from the soft floral design on the patterned paper, to the ribbon, to the colors, to the, well, everything. Journaling sits inside the soft curve of a quarter circle; key words are highlighted white to stand out from the pink. Large chipboard letter and number accents dot the page in a visual triangle, keeping total focus on the photo.

Supplies: Patterned paper (Adorn It, My Mind's Eye); letter stickers (American Crafts, EK Success); large chipboard letter (BasicGrey); chipboard letters, adhesive foam; mesh accent (Magic Mesh); ribbons (American Crafts, Offray); flowers (Teters); buttons; embroidery floss; flower beads (source unknown)

Peek-a-boo
Gift Bag

Amber Baley, Waupun, Wisconsin

Hey, no peeking! This unique gift bag can hint at the treasures inside with its wraparound transparency window (if you want to hide the contents completely, just add fun tissue paper). The bag, created with the help of a template, has the transparency stitched to the inside for extra security.

Supplies: Patterned paper (Fancy Pants Designs, My Mind's Eye); transparency (K & Company); die cut shapes, gift bag pattern (Provo Craft); ribbon (May Arts); button; thread; twine

Card Full of Caring

Amber Baley, Waupun, Wisconsin

Homemade heart accents allure the eye to this card, but the real treasure is the card's dual purpose. The text-patterned transparency, which was sewn to white cardstock, is attached to the card face with just ribbon. That way, it can be removed and used as a Valentine's door hanger. The black text on a white background provides a classic and clear canvas for the dyed chipboard hearts to play across.

Supplies: Transparency (Creative Imaginations); rub-ons (7 Gypsies); die-cut hearts (Provo Craft); ribbon (Offray); dimensional adhesive; acrylic paint; rubber stamp (Hero Arts); stamping ink; chipboard; thread; cardstock

TRANS PARENCY

My Roses

Barb Hogan, Cincinnati, Ohio

A variety of soft, scripted text is paired with a playful, shabby title for a bouquet of stunning typography. The background is built by layering a text-patterned transparency over a background of distressed patterned paper, which offers its own subtle text pattern. Handwritten captions define photos with lines of flirty dark text. The title grabs the eye with strong serifed letters, a mix of upper- and lowercase letters and distressed-effect paint.

Supplies: Transparency (K & Company); patterned paper (source unknown); chipboard letters (Pressed Petals); stamp (Stampin' Up); stamping ink; circle cutter; pen; cardstock

Not Your Ordinary
Bulletin Board

Linda Harrison, Sarasota, Florida

Do you have a child learning their ABCs? Perhaps there's a certain teacher who helped your child learn those little symbols so necessary for life? Maybe you are just fond of words and have a playful spirit. This chalk- and cork-board set satisfies all of the above criteria. These boards are readily available at craft stores and are easy to decorate. Simply paint the frames (if you like the checkerboard pattern, be sure to begin with the lighter paint color first). Once dry, embellish with letters or accents of your choice. These letters are paper die-cuts, but rub-ons, stickers or stamped letters could also be used.

Supplies: Chalkboard, corkboard (Michaels); acrylic paint; die-cut letters (QuickKutz); buttons (Jo-Ann Stores); embroidery floss; pen; cardstock

Happy

Shannon Taylor, Bristol, Tennessee

This layout wraps the reader up in carefree elegance. Sophisticated floral iron-ons speak to the sophistication of a grown-up woman who has what she wants and knows where she is going. Her playful side is expressed through relaxed handwritten journaling that has been cut into strips and placed so the edges of the strips point directly to the photo. The title shows a zesty spirit and is reinforced by a handmade letter accent. A chipboard circle was sanded and inked. Then buttons were added and highlighted with a few strands of embroidery floss.

Supplies: Cardstock; rub-on letters (Imagination Project); flowers (Hirschberg Schutz & Co.); buttons (Blumenthal); embroidery floss; thread; wood tag (Chatterbox); chalk; Jayne Print font (Dafont)

Integrate Text Into Design

- Seek balance by assigning text areas a value. Squint your eyes, look at the page and decide if any text areas appear too heavy or too light.
- Play with proportion and scale. Are you putting enough emphasis on the title? Consider its size in relation to the rest of the page elements.
- Create rhythm by choosing fonts that share similar line and shape qualities (also, be sure that the rest of your layout echoes these qualities).
- Unify the page by choosing fonts that carry the mood of your page. When integrating text into your design, use colors and media that also support the theme.

Let me start by saying in your defense, Honey, that I honestly don't think your collection of watches came as a result of you simply being over-indulgent.

Or materialistic.

Or purposely acquisitive.

No, I really don't think you intentionally set out to own 11 working watches at one time. After all, I truly understand how things like this can happen. You receive one as a Christmas gift from my dad, get one from my brother for your birthday and acquire two in two years as gifts from me. Then you purchase a few others, here and there, while you are out shopping for a new shirt or some cologne.

I completely understand!

And I think that this is a great example of why we are so great together. Because I just know that when someone has a collection of watches like you do, there is no way that you can think anything odd of my 'conservative' collection of shoes.

With
Time to Spare

Linda Harrison, Sarasota, Florida

This title is quite a play on words, as it alludes to the number of watches a certain husband owns (or perhaps we should say, "collects"). With 11, the hubby could probably spare one or two. This design capitalizes on the round shape of a wristwatch. The photos emphasize the round-faced timepieces in the collection, and the photos and journaling are nicely fitted inside a circle, whose edges are made complete with curved blocks of patterned paper. Clock hands direct the eyes to key photos, the journaling and the title.

Supplies: Patterned paper (American Crafts); chipboard letters (Pressed Petals); die-cut letters, clock hands (QuicKutz); brads (Happy Hammer); circle cutter; cardstock; Castorgate Wide, Sans Serif fonts (Microsoft)

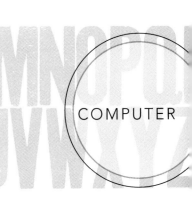

Thinking-of-You Card

Vicki Boutin, Burlington, Ontario, Canada

Bright colors welcome this card's recipient into a world of home-spun thoughtfulness. Layers of coordinating patterned papers are offset by dimensional accents. A chipboard accent spells out the message while a handwritten collection of repeated words reinforces the message of the card.

Supplies: Patterned paper (A2Z Essentials, Imagination Project); chipboard coaster and flower (Imagination Project); button; pen; cardstock

HAND WRITTEN

Men in My Life

Barb Hogan, Cincinnati, Ohio

When creating a digital layout, don't forget that you can always add your handwriting directly to the layout. Simply print the layout and go nuts with the pen. This digital layout offers layers of photos interspersed with beautiful textures. The title was created with a decorative font set at a large point size. Once printed, the artist simply journaled inside the recesses of the outlined letters.

Supplies: Image editing software (Adobe); digital elements (Designer Digitals, Dianne Rigdon); pen; cardstock

Scrapbookers learn to be resourceful early on in their hobby. For instance, should you run out of the letter "d" in your letter sticker collection, the letter "p" turned upside down and backward will work in a pinch. Text-rich travel patterned paper creates a background that breathes subtle whispers of the page theme. Handwritten journaling captions line the photos, adding definition to the page both figuratively and literally.

Supplies: Patterned paper (Karen Foster Design, Paper Studio); letter stickers (Making Memories); ampersand sticker, month sticker (EK Success); pigment ink; pen; cardstock

Brad & Dad

Karen Davis, Hillsboro, Ohio

Source Guide

The following companies manufacture products featured in this book. Please check your local retailers to find these materials, or go to a company's Web site for the latest product. In addition, we have made every attempt to properly credit the items mentioned in this book. We apologize to any company that we have listed incorrectly and would appreciate hearing from you.

7 Gypsies
(877) 749-7797
www.sevengypsies.com

A2Z Essentials
(419) 663-2869
www.geta2z.com

Adobe Systems Incorporated
(800) 833-6687
www.adobe.com

Adorn It/Carolee's Creations
(435) 563-1100
www.adornit.com

All My Memories
(888) 553-1998
www.allmymemories.com

All Night Media — see Plaid Enterprises

American Crafts
(801) 226-0747
www.americancrafts.com

Anna Griffin, Inc.
(888) 817-8170
www.annagriffin.com

Arctic Frog
(479) 636-3764
www.arcticfrog.com

Autumn Leaves
(800) 588-6707
www.autumnleaves.com

BasicGrey
(801) 544-1116
www.basicgrey.com

Bazzill Basics Paper
(480) 558-8557
www.bazzillbasics.com

Beadery, The
(401) 539-2432
www.thebeadery.com

Berwick Offray, LLC
(800) 344-5533
www.offray.com

Blumenthal Lansing Company
(563) 538-4211
www.buttonsplus.com

Bo-Bunny Press
(801) 771-4010
www.bobunny.com

Carolee's Creations — see Adorn It

Chatterbox, Inc.
(888) 416-6260
www.chatterboxinc.com

Cherry Arte
(212) 465-3495
www.cherryarte.com

Clearsnap, Inc.
(888) 448-4862
www.clearsnap.com

Cosmo Cricket
(800) 852-8810
www.cosmocricket.com

Crate Paper
(702) 966-0409
www.cratepaper.com

Creative Imaginations
(800) 942-6487
www.cigift.com

Creative Paper Co. — no source available

Dafont
www.dafont.com

Daisy D's Paper Company
(888) 601-8955
www.daisydspaper.com

DecoArt Inc.
(800) 367-3047
www.decoart.com

Delta Technical Coatings, Inc.
(800) 423-4135
www.deltacrafts.com

Deluxe Designs
(480) 497-9005
www.deluxecuts.com

DesignerDigitals
www.designerdigitals.com

Dianne Rigdon, Shabby Elements
www.shabbyelements.com

Die Cuts With A View
(801) 224-6766
www.diecutswithaview.com

Doodlebug Design Inc.
(877) 800-9190
www.doodlebug.ws

EK Success, Ltd.
(800) 524-1349
www.eksuccess.com

Fancy Pants Designs, LLC
(801) 779-3212
www.fancypantsdesigns.com

Fiskars, Inc.
(866) 348-5661
www.fiskars.com

FontWerks
(604) 942-3105
www.fontwerks.com

Fossil
(800) 449-3056
www.fossil.com

Gel-a-tins inc.
(800) 393-2151
www.gelatinstamps.com

Go West Studios
(214) 227-0007
www.goweststudios.com

Grafix
(800) 447-2349
www.grafixarts.com

Hambly Studios
(800) 451-3999
www.hamblystudios.com

Happy Hammer, The
(720) 870-5248
www.thehappyhammer.com

Harold's Fonts
www.haroldsfonts.com

Heidi Grace Designs, Inc.
(866) 348-5661
www.heidigrace.com

Heidi Swapp/Advantus Corporation
(904) 482-0092
www.heidiswapp.com

Hero Arts Rubber Stamps, Inc.
(800) 822-4376
www.heroarts.com

Hirschberg Schutz & Co., Inc.
(800) 221-8640

Imagination Project, Inc.
(888) 477-6532
www.imaginationproject.com

Jo-Ann Stores
www.joann.com

Junkitz
(732) 792-1108
www.junkitz.com

K&Company
(888) 244-2083
www.kandcompany.com

Karen Foster Design
(801) 451-9779
www.karenfosterdesign.com

Kathy Moore
www.digidivadesigns.com

KI Memories
(972) 243-5595
www.kimemories.com

Lä Dé Dä
(225) 755-8899
www.ladeda.com

Li'l Davis Designs
(480) 223-0080
www.lildavisdesigns.com

Magic Mesh
(651) 345-6374
www.magicmesh.com

Making Memories
(801) 294-0430
www.makingmemories.com

May Arts
(800) 442-3950
www.mayarts.com

Maya Road, LLC
(214) 488-3279
www.mayaroad.com

Melissa Frances/Heart & Home, Inc.
(888) 616-6166
www.melissafrances.com

Memories Complete, LLC
(866) 966-6365
www.memoriescomplete.com

Michael Miller Memories
(646) 230-8862
www.michaelmillermemories.com

Michaels Arts & Crafts
(800) 642-4235
www.michaels.com

Microsoft Corporation
www.microsoft.com

My Mind's Eye, Inc.
(866) 989-0320
www.mymindseye.com

My Sentiments Exactly
(719) 260-6001
www.sentiments.com

Nunn Design
(800) 761-3557
www.nunndesign.com

Offray — see Berwick Offray, LLC

Paper Studio
(480) 557-5700
www.paperstudio.com

Pebbles Inc.
(801) 235-1520
www.pebblesinc.com

Pixie Press
www.hsn.com

Plaid Enterprises, Inc.
(800) 842-4197
www.plaidonline.com

Polar Bear Press
(801) 451-7670
www.polarbearpress.com

Pressed Petals
(800) 748-4656
www.pressedpetals.com

Prima Marketing, Inc.
(909) 627-5532
www.primamarketinginc.com

Provo Craft
(800) 937-7686
www.provocraft.com

Queen & Co.
(858) 613-7858
www.queenandcompany.com

QuicKutz, Inc.
(888) 702-1146
www.quickutz.com

Ranger Industries, Inc.
(800) 244-2211
www.rangerink.com

Rhonna Designs
www.rhonnadesigns.com

Rocky Mountain Scrapbook Co.
(801) 731-5657
www.rmscrapbook.com

Rusty Pickle
(801) 746-1045
www.rustypickle.com

Sandylion Sticker Designs
(800) 387-4215
www.sandylion.com

Scenic Route Paper Co.
(801) 225-5754
www.scenicroutepaper.com

Scrap Supply
(615) 777-3953
www.scrapsupply.com

Scrapworks, LLC/As You Wish Products, LLC
(801) 363-1010
www.scrapworks.com

SEI, Inc.
(800) 333-3279
www.shopsei.com

Shabby Princess
www.shabbyprincess.com

Shoebox Trims
(303) 257-7578
www.shoeboxtrims.com

Something Blue Studios
www.somethingbluestudios.com

Stampa Rosa — no source available

Stampin' Up!
(800) 782-6787
www.stampinup.com

Strano Designs
(508) 454-4615
www.stranodesigns.com

Technique Tuesday, LLC
(503) 644-4073
www.techniquetuesday.com

Teters Floral Products
(800) 999-5996
www.teters.com

Therm O Web, Inc.
(800) 323-0799
www.thermoweb.com

Tsukineko, Inc.
(800) 769-6633
www.tsukineko.com

Two Peas in a Bucket
(888) 896-7327
www.twopeasinabucket.com

Urban Lily
www.urbanlily.com

vLetter, Inc.
(541) 387-2800
www.vletter.com

Wal-Mart Stores, Inc.
www.walmart.com

We R Memory Keepers, Inc.
(801) 539-5000
www.weronthenet.com

Westrim Crafts
(800) 727-2727
www.westrimcrafts.com

Zsiage, LLC
(718) 224-1976
www.zsiage.com

Index

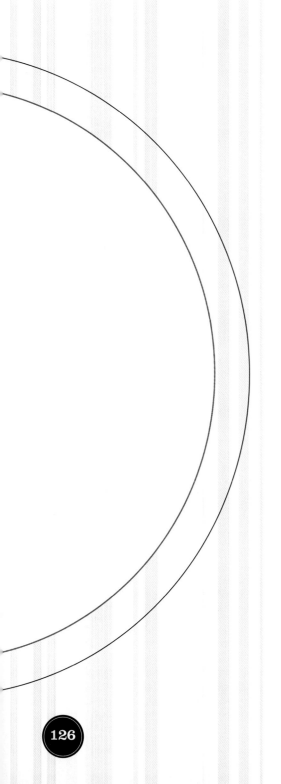

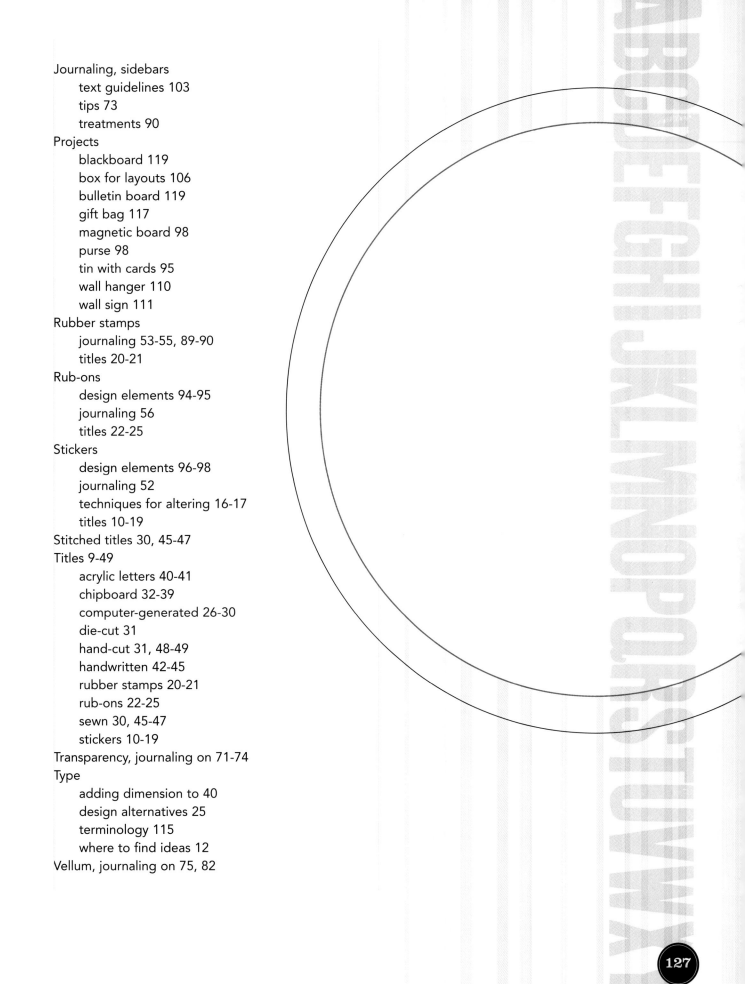

Check Out More Great Books from Memory Makers!

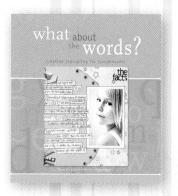

Over 30 unique journaling formats and page after page of great layouts will inspire scrapbookers to record their own memories and experiences in the most engaging and expressive ways possible.

ISBN-13: 978-1-892127-77-8
ISBN-10: 1-892127-77-6

paperback
128 pages

Z0017

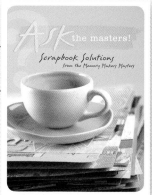

Get solutions for fifty scrapbooking challenges and problems from our team of experts—the Memory Makers Masters. Be inspired by a gallery of full-color scrapbook pages.

ISBN-13: 978-1-892127-88-4
ISBN-10: 1-892127-88-1

paperback
128 pages

Z0277

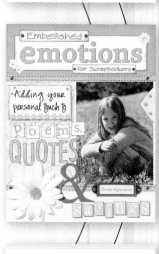

Learn from scrapbook artist Trudy Sigurdson about how to begin a journey into capturing emotion on scrapbook pages through the use of poems, quotes and sayings.

ISBN-13: 978-1-892127-84-6
ISBN-10: 1-892127-84-9

paperback
112 pages

Z0023

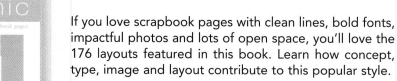

If you love scrapbook pages with clean lines, bold fonts, impactful photos and lots of open space, you'll love the 176 layouts featured in this book. Learn how concept, type, image and layout contribute to this popular style.

ISBN-13: 978-1-892127-78-5
ISBN-10: 1-892127-78-4

paperback
128 pages

Z0018